DADDY'S HOME
by
Ivan Menchell

DADDY'S HOME was produced in New York at the Nat Horne Theatre as part of the Eleventh Double Image Annual Short Play Festival on May 2 and 4, 1986. The production was directed by Gitta Honegger, dramaturged by David Moore, and stage managed by Heidi Schultz. The scenery and costumes were designed by Tina Cantu Navarro; the lighting was designed by Clay Shirky. The cast was as follows:

DAVID .... David Officer

JOAN .... Deborah Hecht

DADDY'S HOME was originally presented at the Yale School of Drama in December, 1984. The production was directed by Ethan Ruber, dramaturged by David Moore, designed by Jim Sandefur, and stage managed by Peggy Vernieu. The cast was as follows:

DAVID .... Anders Bolang

JOAN .... Gail Dartez

The author is grateful to have studied with Howard Stein, Leon Katz, Jay Novick, Oscar Brownstein, and Bill Pfister, and to have had their guidence and support through the years.

OFF-OFF BROADWAY FESTIVAL PLAYS
ELEVENTH SERIES

Selected by New York theatre critics and the editorial staff of Samuel French, Inc., as the most important plays in the Eleventh Annual Off-Off Broadway Original Short Play Festival, sponsored by Double Image Theatre, Inc.

DADDY'S HOME
by Ivan Menchell

RECENSIO: a light and dark show
by Eddie De Santis

THE TIES THAT BIND
by Matthew Witten

GHOST STORIES
by Annie Evans

SAMUEL FRENCH, INC.
45 West 25th Street NEW YORK 10010
7623 Sunset Boulevard HOLLYWOOD 90046
LONDON TORONTO

ISBN 0 573 68909 1

Printed in U.S.A

For Mom, Roland, and Mollie
and for the home we left behind.

/ / /

Be it ever so broken,
there's no place like home.

DADDY'S HOME

SETTING: The play takes place in JOAN SINGER'S house, in a suburb of New York. The stage is split in half: on the right side is JOAN'S bedroom and on the left is her son, DAVID'S. The two rooms are separated by a hallway with the entrance to JOAN'S upstage and the entrance to DAVID'S downstage. Both rooms are a mess though DAVID'S is clearly in far more turmoil. Clothing and belongings are all over the place. Some things are in boxes, but most await packing. There is a full length mirror in JOAN'S room, a large cassette player/radio in DAVID'S, and a telephone in both.

AT RISE: DAVID, aged sixteen, sits on his bed. He has just finished talking on the phone. He slams down the receiver.

DAVID. Asshole! Stupid asshole! ... Just try and come by now... After we move I'll take all this shit and just pile it up in front of my door. Even if you come by you won't be able to get in. You'll have to pound and pound and pound and beg and plead ... but I'll have it all piled up high ... right up to the ceiling. You'll need a fucking army to get through the door... They'll pound and pound away and I won't even answer. They'll try battering rams and all kinds of shit, but nothing'll work... You'll just pound and pound away 'till there's no other choice... You'll have to blow up the door. You'll have to put dynamite all over the place ... and then, finally, when it blows and everything comes crashing down ... I'll be lying in bed pretending I'm asleep... *(He runs to his bed and lies down as if he's asleep. He then falls off the bed from the impact of "the explosion" and "wakes up" to play the following.)*

Oh, hi Dad. I didn't hear you come in.

(As his father.)
What do you mean, you didn't hear me come in? I've been pounding and pounding and pounding!

(As himself.)
No kidding. I must've been out like a light. What's the army for, Dad?

(As his father.)
I needed them to blow up the door!

(As himself.)
Yeh, I see. Wow, Mom's going to be real pissed off when she gets home.

(As his father.)
To hell with your mother! Now let's go. Today's Sunday and you're going out with me!

(As himself.)
Gee Dad, I'd really like to but I'm kind of tired and besides, I promised Mom I'd hang around the house today.

(As his father.)
I said you're coming out with me!

(As himself.)
And I said I'm not, so why don't you just beat it before I knock you apart with my ... *(He looks around the room for a weapon and decides on a baseball bat.)* ... With my heat seeking thermonuclear, Anti-Asshole Warhead!

(As his father.)
Oh no! Not the heat seeking, thermonuclear, Anti-Asshole Warhead!

(As himself.)
I'll count to three, then you and the army better be gone ... One ... two...

(As his father.)
We're going! We're going!

(He runs out the door and up the hallway, first as his father, then as himself firing after his father. He then re-enters his room and starts swinging the baseball bat. He tosses a record cover on the floor to make a home plate. stepping up to the "plate," he waits for the pitch The imaginary ball is thrown, and DAVID slams it way out into "the field." He watches the ball with pride then quickly throws down the bat, puts on his baseball glove and runs back for the catch yelling "I got it ... I got it." He makes a brilliant catch, then makes crowd cheering sounds followed by an announcement in a loud voice.)

The Spring Valley Lions have won the Little League Championship!!

(He grabs his trophy and waves it high in the air. More cheering. After a moment he stops and throws the glove and the trophy on the floor.)

Jesus Christ, what am I going to do with all this shit?

(He spots some old books on the floor, picks them up and reads the titles.)

The Red Steam Engine, Winnie The Pooh, The Little Prince.

(Reads the inscription.) "To David, you'll always be *our* Little Prince. We love you, Mommy and Daddy." *(Opens another book and reads.)* "Happy birthday Champ, love Daddy ..." Christ, she can take them if she wants. *(He gathers up the books, exits his room, walks up the hallway and enters JOAN'S. Noticing a picture of his father on her dresser, he picks it up and speaks to it.)* Asshole ... Dick wad. *(He replaces the picture and sets the books down next to it. Since he's got the house to himself, he decides to search through his mother's belongings. While carefully looking through her suitcase he comes across one of her brassieres. He picks it up and holds it in the air.)* Not bad, Mom ... Hook in the back, easy access. *(He puts his arms through it, wraps it around his chest, then lets it pop open. Imitating his mother.)* I beg your pardon. What on earth do you think you're doing? My son's in the very next room. How dare you even try such a thing!

(From offstage JOAN is heard yelling "I'm back.")

(To himself.) Shit! *(He quickly takes off the brassiere, puts it back in the suitcase and runs to his room. Yelling down the hallway.)* I'm up in my room. *(He pretends to be packing as JOAN comes down the hallway carrying large cartons. She is in her mid-forties.)*

JOAN. *(Entering his room.)* This was all I could get. We'll just have to make do. I don't think it will be too bad, though. *(She sets a few cartons down. Ironically.)* I see you've made enormous strides.

DAVID. The phone hasn't stopped ringing. Everybody's been calling to say goodbye. My whole class must've called while you were out. I swear.

JOAN. Did Daddy call?

DAVID. Uh ... no.

JOAN. Well, let's see if we can keep off the phone for a while and get some work done, okay?

DAVID. Sure.

(JOAN begins to exit. The PHONE RINGS. She stops.)

DAVID. I'll get it. *(Answering the phone.)* Hello.

JOAN. Is it Daddy?

DAVID. No.

JOAN. Well make it short. *(She exits his room, walks up the hallway and enters her room.)*

DAVID. *(on the phone)* So how you doing? ... Supposed to be around seven but I'm sure we won't be out of here before twelve.

JOAN. *(to herself)* Just look at this stuff.

DAVID. So what's going on with you?...

JOAN. There's no end. There's just no end.

DAVID. Yeh, but listen, I should tell you that even Arthur got to third base with Robin so it's not much of an accomplishment...

JOAN. *(She stands by her bed and begins sorting out the pile of dresses that lay in front of her. She tosses the ones she doesn't want on the floor.)* I wish I had a dollar for every dress that's gone out of fashion.

DAVID. Well, if you can get down Tracy's pants, *then* you've got something.

JOAN. I wish I had a dollar for every dress that doesn't fit anymore.

DAVID. Well, she told John to drop dead, get lost, and leave her alone, but he's not giving up. He says he can read between the lines.

JOAN. *(Holding up a dress.)* I couldn't have worn this in public. *(She throws it on to the pile on the floor.)*

DAVID. I don't think so. I heard Tommy went out with her and she wouldn't even let him get under her shirt.

JOAN. *(She picks out an emerald green dress, holds it against herself and looks in the mirror.)* My God, you were quite a knockout once, Joan.

DAVID. I know. I guess some girls just aren't sexually mature.

JOAN. *(Yelling over to DAVID.)* David, get off the phone and finish packing.

DAVID. *(Yelling back.)* In a sec. *(on the phone)* But listen, don't let it discourage you. Go for it. Maybe you're the one who can get her to *open up* ... I mean, she's got to give in sooner or later. It's only a matter of time ... *(JOAN exits her bedroom and walks to DAVID'S.)* No, I'm going after Ellen ... So who cares if she's a little cross eyed. All I know is that she's got the biggest set of tits in the tenth grade ... *(He spots JOAN standing in the doorway.)* Listen, I gotta go. I'll call you back in a little while.

JOAN. You're not calling anyone.

DAVID. I'll talk to you later. *(He hangs up the phone.)*

JOAN. Is that all you and your friends talk about, tits?

DAVID. What else are we supposed to talk about?

JOAN. Politics, world affairs, the economy.

DAVID. Oh Mom, be serious. I'm sure you talked about the same things when you were a kid. I mean, about guys and stuff.

JOAN. Not the way you and your friends do.

DAVID. Oh come on. Think back, *way* back.

JOAN. Very funny. Let me tell you something: there is more to a woman, a girl, than breasts.

DAVID. You haven't seen Ellen.

JOAN. It may seem hard to believe but there are other qualities just as important. I'm sure even Ellen has many fine attributes other than possessing the largest knockers God has bestowed upon a tenth grader.

DAVID. I'm looking for them, I swear.

JOAN. We'll carry on this conversation another time. Now please sort this stuff out. Before you know it you'll be too tired to finish, and I can tell you right now that whatever isn't packed up by the time the moving men ring that bell tomorrow morning is staying behind and getting thrown out. Now stay off the phone and get organized. Have I made myself clear?

DAVID. Are you in a bad mood?

JOAN. Don't start with me, David. *(She exits DAVID'S room, then enters hers.)*

DAVID. *(To himself.)* She's in a bad mood. Next, she'll start getting hot.

JOAN. *(Yelling over to DAVID.)* David, did you turn up the heat?

DAVID. *(Yelling back.)* No.

JOAN. Don't you find it warm?

DAVID. No.

JOAN. Well, maybe if you did a little work instead of talking on the phone all night you'd get a little warm.

DAVID. *(To himself, mimicking her.)* Well, maybe if you did a little work instead of talking on the phone all night you'd get a little warm.

JOAN. *(To herself.)* Why doesn't somebody abolish adolescence?

DAVID. She better grow out of this phase real soon. *(He switches on the cassette player, and music begins blaring. He picks up the tennis racket, pretends it's a guitar and begins miming wildly to the song. Upon hearing the noise, JOAN stands for a moment listening in disbelief, then exits her room and walks to DAVID'S. His back is to the door so he does not see her standing there. She watches for a moment caught between anger and amusement then switches off the music. DAVID freezes, then turns to her. Mockingly.)* That's how you shut it off? I'm in here racking my brains trying to figure out how to turn that darn thing off. You mean to tell me you knew all the time and waited 'till now to show me? Not very considerate Mom, that's all I have to say. Not very considerate ... You better get cracking. Before you know it you'll be too tired to finish.

JOAN. Thank you. Now, can we keep the noise level in here down to something that won't register on a Richter scale. I want to call Daddy. *(She starts to leave. DAVID stops her.)*

DAVID. It's going to be great living in the city.

JOAN. I know.

DAVID. Just think how much easier it'll be for you. I mean, you won't have to worry about me so much.

JOAN. Oh, I won't?

DAVID. No. I mean, I'll be able to take care of myself. I'll get a job.

JOAN. Oh my God!

DAVID. Yeh. I'll make my own money. You won't have to give me any, and you won't have to drive me everywhere like you do here. I'll be able to walk or take the train. Just think how much easier it'll be for you ... and now my curfew won't have to be so early.

JOAN. Oh really?

DAVID. Yeh. I mean, I am getting older, you know. Twelve o'clock is a little early for a sixteen-year-old, especially in Manhattan.

JOAN. Oh, you think so?

DAVID. Sure. I think one o'clock would be fair. One-thirty on weekends.

JOAN. Don't get your hopes up.

DAVID. Why not?

JOAN. This is no time to discuss it.

DAVID. Sure it is.

JOAN. The discussion is closed. *(She exits DAVID'S room and walks to hers. He follows.*

DAVID. Give me one good reason—

JOAN. David!

DAVID. Okay, Jesus.

JOAN. Just because we're moving it does not mean we are making radical changes in our lifestyle.

DAVID. Since when is coming in an hour later a radical change?

JOAN. Since I said so.

DAVID. You know, just because you're the parent and I'm the kid doesn't mean you can make decisions like that without a good reason.

JOAN. What you don't seem to understand is that just *because* I'm the parent and you're the kid is reason enough.

DAVID. You're right, this is not time to discuss it.

JOAN. Watch it.

DAVID. I don't know what you're worried about *me* for. I mean, think of how busy *you're* going to be. The city is where all the action is. There's got to be tons of eligible bachelors just looking for an attractive, intelligent, older woman. You'll probably be out every night.

JOAN. I'm glad you think so.

DAVID. In fact, I think the real question here is what time *your* curfew is going to be.

JOAN. We'll cross that bridge when we come to it.

DAVID. And if you're not coming in at night I expect you to call.

JOAN. All right, enough.

DAVID. I'm only—

JOAN. Enough! *(pause)* I'm sorry if I've been a little short tempered with you this evening.

DAVID. Don't worry about it, I understand. *(Referring to*

the dresses on the floor.) What are you doing with those?

JOAN. I'm giving them away.

DAVID. Don't you like them anymore?

JOAN. It's not a question of me liking them but of them liking me.

DAVID. What, did you have a fight with them or something?

JOAN. I've outgrown them.

DAVID. What are you talking about? You stopped growing a thousand years ago.

JOAN. Thank you.

DAVID. You know what I mean.

JOAN. Let's just say they don't flatter me the way they used to. *(DAVID picks out the emerald green dress from the pile. He holds it up.)*

DAVID. But you used to love this one. You said it showed off your eyes.

JOAN. Unfortunately, it now shows off too much of everything else.

DAVID. I'll bet it still looks great.

JOAN. You'd lose.

DAVID. Bet you I wouldn't. Go ahead, try it on.

JOAN. Stop it.

DAVID. No, I'm telling you, it'll look great. Trust me.

JOAN. Trust you?

DAVID. Yeh. I know what looks good on a girl.

JOAN. Oh you do, do you?

DAVID. Sure. I mean, after all, when a girl gets dressed up what's she dressing up for? To impress a man, and speaking as a man I can guarantee that that dress'll turn a lot of heads.

JOAN. Oh, it will?

DAVID. I'm telling you ... You used to wear it all the time when you went out with Dad.

JOAN. I did wear other dresses too, you know. I do own a few.

DAVID. Yeh, but that's the one you wore to fancy places when Dad wanted to show you off.

JOAN. When he wanted to show me off?

DAVID. You know what I mean.

JOAN. Where on earth did you come up with that idea?

DAVID. He used to say it all the time. *(Mimicking his father.)* "Honey, put on the green dress. I want to really show you off tonight." *(JOAN laughs.)* Right?

JOAN. Look, even if I could get it on I'd probably need a crow bar to get it off.

DAVID. Don't worry about it. If you have any problems, I'll call the fire department. Who knows, maybe you could get lucky. Firemen are pretty neat guys.

JOAN. When I need a matchmaker, I'll call you.

DAVID. Just trying to help.

JOAN. Go finish your room.

DAVID. I'm telling you—

JOAN. David.

DAVID. Okay, I'm going, I'm going. *(He exits JOAN'S room and goes to his. JOAN is left holding the green dress. After a moment she decides to try it on. As she changes, DAVID comes across an old stuffed rabbit. He holds it up and speaks to it.)*

DAVID. Well, I guess this is it. I'd love to take you with me, but let's face it — what's a girl going to think when I bring her back to my room and she sees you sitting around? It's not going to look too good. *(He throws the rabbit into a carton. After a moment he retrieves it.)* I'll tell you what I'll do. I'll give you to my cousin. Andy'll take real good care of you ... and I'll come and visit you on weekends .. every weekend. *(He sits on the bed. Pause.)* What'll happen is I'll come by every weekend for the first couple of months or so. After that I'll start coming every two weeks. I mean, there's going to be times when I just can't come over. I got my own life to lead. I can't give up every goddamn weekend. You're just going to have to be a man about this.

(JOAN has got the dress on and is looking at herself in the full length mirror. She struggles to make the dress look as good as possible but it is simply too tight.)

JOAN. Face it Joan, you're getting too old for slits ... although emerald green does highlight the varicose veins.

DAVID. Like I said, what's a girl going to think when I bring her back and she sees you sitting around? She's going to think "what's this pain in the ass kid doing here?" That's what she's going to think.

JOAN. Maybe I should give it to Joan Collins. She could wear it on *Dynasty* as a little something she threw on for breakfast.

DAVID. Now you wouldn't want to cramp my style would you? ... I didn't think so.

JOAN. *(As Joan Collins in Dynasty.)* Good morning darling. What did you say your names was? ... Oh, you like it?

It's just a little something I threw on for breakfast. *(DAVID takes the stuffed rabbit, exits his room and walks to JOAN'S. She is enjoying the role.)* The only question that keeps running through my mind is was it as good for *me* as it was for you?

DAVID. *(from the hallway)* Mom, listen, there's a lot of stuff — *(He stops in the doorway, then puts the rabbit on the bed. Pause.)*

JOAN. Don't say a word. *(pause)*

DAVID. It still looks good.

JOAN. You think so?

DAVID. Did it shrink?

JOAN. David!

(The phone rings.)

DAVID. I'll get it.

JOAN. *I'll* get it. *(Answering the phone.)* Hello ... Oh hello, Ellen...

DAVID. I'll take it in my room.

JOAN. *(on the phone)* No, I'm sorry, he's busy packing. I'll have him call you when he's finished. Goodbye.

DAVID. What did you do that for?

JOAN. You've got work to do.

DAVID. Thanks a lot.

JOAN. When you're done you can talk all you want.

DAVID. Okay, then when your friends call I'll tell them the same thing.

JOAN. Don't threaten me.

DAVID. Oh, but it's okay for you to threaten me.

JOAN. It seems the only way to get through to you.

DAVID. Look, I'll finish packing after I talk to Ellen.

JOAN. I said you're not talking to anyone. Now go finish your room

DAVID. I don't believe you. This is stupid. Look, I'll just be a few minutes. It's an important call.

JOAN. It will just have to wait.

DAVID. *(walking out)* Fine! Then I'm not telling you when Daddy's calling back.

JOAN. *(following him)* Your father called?!

DAVID. *(entering his room)* Maybe, maybe not.

JOAN. So help me, I will knock you right through that wall if you don't tell me right now! *(pause)*

DAVID. He called while you were out getting boxes.

JOAN. What did he want? What did he say?

DAVID. He said that you should let me call Ellen.

JOAN. What did he want?

DAVID. He wanted to wish us luck with the move. *(JOAN walks back to her room, picks up the phone and dials. David exits his room and walks slowly up the hallway.)* He's not home. *(He enters her room.)*

JOAN. Where is he? *(Pause. Hanging up the phone.)* Where is he?

DAVID. He's out.

JOAN. Out where?

DAVID. He went out for dinner with what's-her-name.

JOAN. Sharon.

DAVID. Yeh. He said he'd call back at ten. *(pause)*

JOAN. Why did I have to do that? Why do you make me lose my temper?

DAVID. Oh, I suppose it's my fault.

JOAN. Yes.

DAVID. Look, just because you're in a bad mood don't—

JOAN. I am not in a bad mood. I was fine until you started.

DAVID. Who are you kidding? You've been like this ever since the house was sold.

JOAN. Don't be ridiculous. I've thanked God every night that we've finally found a buyer for this house. You think this year's been fun? You think this year's been easy? You think I enjoy knowing that at six o'clock I won't hear the sound of a key turning in the front door? You think I enjoy having to concentrate on setting the table for two because when I don't a third place seems to pop up? You think I enjoy coming back to this room every night having to ... Why didn't you tell me Daddy called? I asked you when I came in. Why did you lie to me?

DAVID. 'Cause I didn't want you going crazy all night waiting for him to call.

JOAN. Is that what you thought, that I'd go crazy? ... Very nice ... I will thank you next time to tell me when Daddy calls and let me be the judge as to whether or not it will drive me crazy. Is that understood?

DAVID. Yes.

JOAN. Good. Now we have a lot of work to do. I suggest we both get cracking. *(DAVID exits and goes to his room. JOAN takes one last look at herself in the mirror. She makes one last attempt with the dress then takes it off and throws it on the pile on the floor. By this point DAVID has entered his room and begun throwing his things into boxes.)*

DAVID. I don't need this shit, any of it! I'm moving to a

new place with new things and I don't need any of your shit! Now me and Mom are going to be living somewhere that's *ours* ... a place that has nothing to do with you! We're leaving all your goddamn shit ... your goddamn home ... everything! ... So I don't need your bat, your glove, your stupid radio, your lousy games, none of it!

JOAN. *(She has come across an old photo album. She looks through the pictures.)* What do you know ... I wonder if you're smiling because we're going camping or because you just came back from that little tart you're fucking now. I hope she breaks your back.

DAVID. I'll take the stuff *I* want. My *own* stuff, stuff *I* bought! *(He looks around the room but can't find anything. He then remembers his pornographic magazine collection. He lifts up his mattress, takes out the magazines and makes himself comfortable on the bed as he sorts through them.)*

JOAN. You know what your problem is, Dan? ... You're a schmuck. You weren't when we first met. It was something that developed gradually.

DAVID. *(Opening one of the magazines.)* Let's see. Who do we have here? ... Jenny. Sweet, adorable Jenny. I wouldn't dream of deserting you. Your tits are too good to leave behind.

JOAN. I never thought you'd be the I'm-leaving-an-attractive-intelligent-woman-like-you-for-a-somewhat-cute-yet-mentally-incompetent-little-girl-type.

DAVID. *(Opening another magazine.)* And heeeeeere's Tammy. *(reading)* Who likes good movies, soft music and muscular men ... I guess we just weren't made for each other, Tam.

JOAN. *(She discovers an empty packet of birth control pills that she had once saved and put in the album.)* What do you know ... Well, no more worrying if they did the trick this month. It all takes care of itself now. I can go anywhere at any time and never have to worry about a goddamn thing. I'm always protected! I don't even have a choice ... So these can go right with that emerald green dress. *(She throws the packet onto the pile of dresses, then sorts through more things.)*

DAVID. *(Opening another magazine.)* Ah, my favorite ... Suzanne in the open fields. Now, you look like an intelligent girl. You think it's too much for a guy to get a feel on the first date? I mean, she could do whatever she wanted to me. It's only fair ... Why is it guys aren't hung up on that like girls are? You never hear a guy telling a girl she's going too far or saying "I don't think it's right." I mean, it just doesn't happen ... I bet you never turned a guy down. Just look at you. *(He lies down on his back and holds the centerfold above him. As he enjoys the picture, JOAN spots the stuffed rabbit he placed on her bed earlier. She picks it up and walks to DAVID'S room. Pressing the centerfold against himself.)* I bet you'd really know how to treat a guy. You'd take me in your arms, run your fingers through my hair, kiss my mouth, my neck, my chest, licking your way down ... down .. 'til Whammo!

JOAN. *(standing in the doorway, unseen by DAVID)* What are you doing?

DAVID. Nothing. *(He bolts up, collects the magazines, and dumps them into the nearest carton.)*

JOAN. This is what you've been doing? This is what you're packing?

DAVID. I was just—

JOAN. This is what growing up is? Throwing away everything that's meant something to you, to the family? Throwing away things that were given with love? Throwing away memories and packing up some lousy porno magazine?! *(She throws the rabbit on the bed and pulls out the magazines.)* This is your new life?!

DAVID. I was just going through *all* my stuff.

JOAN. Oh ... Oh, I'm sorry. I forgot. You're a man now. A man doesn't need any of his old things. A man doesn't need to keep beautiful things once he's outgrown them. All a man needs is this. To look at tits! You're a hundred-percent right. Leave everything else behind. This is all that matters. Take the girls with you! *(She begins ripping up the magazines and throwing the pages around the room.)* Here.

DAVID. Stop.

JOAN. Take them all with you!

DAVID. Stop it!

JOAN. We'll get huge boxes so you can take all your huge tits! You can fill your room with them. Wall-to-wall tits!

DAVID. Stop it! Stop it!

JOAN. You disgust me! *(She throws the magazines at him.)*

DAVID. *(picking them up)* Look, just because you're going through the changes don't take it out on me!

JOAN. Why you —

DAVID. Yeh, I know all about it. Hot, cold, yelling. No wonder Dad left. Who the hell can live with you?!

JOAN. You're right. Pack your stuff and get out! *(pause)* Well, what are you waiting for? ... Oh, I forgot. You don't know how to pack. You've grown up and become a man and you don't know how to pack. Well let me show you. *(She begins throwing all his clothes into the duffle bag.)* Now watch carefully because this is something you should know how to do. Now that you've become a man you've got to learn how to throw all your things together and leave the house. Didn't your father teach you anything?!

DAVID. No, he was too busy fighting with his wife!

JOAN. You really think you know everything, don't you? Well, let me tell you something you don't know: living with an adolescent little brat who thinks he's all grown up is a disgusting experience. And I will tell you two things you do not know: the world does not revolve around you, nor does it revolve around tits!

DAVID. You're more hung up on tits than I am.

JOAN. Don't be stupid.

DAVID. Look, I don't know what your problem is.

JOAN. Watch your mouth!

DAVID. No! You come in here like some goddamn—

JOAN. I am still your mother! I don't want to hear that mouth of yours!

DAVID. You don't want to hear anything!

JOAN. Not until you learn to show some respect!

DAVID. I'll show it when you deserve it! *(She slaps him across the face. Pause.)*

JOAN. Do I deserve it now? *(pause)* Is that what I have to do? *(pause)* Is that part of our new life together? *(Pause. Crying.)* Damn it, answer me! Is this our new life together?! *(She exits and goes to her room. There is a moment as they both stand in their rooms. DAVID then slowly walks to JOAN'S room. He stands silently in the doorway as JOAN stands by the bed. Her back to him.)* What do you want? *(pause)*

DAVID. I don't know.

JOAN. I thought you knew everything. *(DAVID starts down the hallway. She calls him back.)* David, come here. I want to show you something. *(He returns to her room. JOAN takes out a snap shot from the album and hands to him. He looks at it.)*

DAVID. Who is she?

JOAN. *(quietly)* Not bad, huh? Nice body, cute little bikini. What do you think? ... What do you think? *(DAVID walks over to the stool by the mirror and sits down.)*

DAVID. Mom.

JOAN. Don't be afraid. Go ahead, tell me. She's not bad, right? ... Right?

DAVID. She's nice.

JOAN. Got great breasts ... Well they are, aren't they? ... Wouldn't *you* say she's got nice tits? ... I'm asking you a question. Don't you think—

DAVID. Yes! ... Yes. Who is she?

JOAN. Funny, how twenty years changes a woman, isn't it? You don't even recognize her now.

DAVID. This picture is you?

JOAN. You see, the whole world does not revolve around tits, because when it does it falls apart, and after it falls apart you have to leave. You have to pack up all your things and move to another world. *(Pause. She sits on the bed.)* It's easy for you to leave, isn't it?

DAVID. I guess.

JOAN. It's exciting to go to a new school, meet new girls, live in Manhattan.

DAVID. There'll be stuff I'll miss.

JOAN. Like what?

DAVID. I don't know. Stuff.

JOAN. I'm going to miss stuff, too ... a lot of stuff I won't have again.

DAVID. Sure you will. And whatever we want that's here we can pack and take.

JOAN. How can I pack? How do I take what's here? ... I want to take the times Daddy used to call me when he was working in the garage just to show me some new gadget he built. I want to take the times we went away together, the times he used to follow you to first base with a movie camera in his hand.

DAVID. God, that was embarrassing.

JOAN. I want to pack up the way he used to go down to the basement every night after dinner and play that little electric organ. Every week he'd learn a new song, and each one sounded worse than the one before. You remember how we used to turn the radio on upstairs to drown out the sound? How do I pack that? *(DAVID gets up and sits beside her on the bed.)* I even want to take the way his work pants always used to drop below his waist and leave his underwear hanging out. I never understood how his pants could slide down while his drawers crept up. How many times I used to yell at him for walking around the house that way when there were people over. I hated that. It made him look so untidy ... It's funny, I see so much of Daddy in you. Your smile, your sense of humor, even the way you walk around the house reminds me of your father. You're getting so tall, so independent ... You really are becoming a man now. You're going to be the man of the house ... I want to pack it all away. I want it all back, everything we had ... but there's no room for it in the new apartment. There's too much stuff, too many things that won't fit ... They belong here. This is where they should stay.

DAVID. What are you talking about?

JOAN. This is where everything belongs. This is where *we* belong.

DAVID. Mom.

JOAN. We can tell them that we changed our minds.

DAVID. No.

JOAN. We could make *this* our new home.

DAVID. No. No! It's Daddy's not ours.

JOAN. It could be. We'll make it ours, yours and mine. We can redecorate. We can change whatever we want. Think how much fun—

DAVID. No! I'm not going to stay here. I'm not! *(He goes back to his room. JOAN follows.)*

JOAN. Can't you see? It's the moving that's making all the problems.

DAVID. It has nothing to do with the moving! It's Daddy! It's your room and my room and the den and the kitchen and the livingroom and I'm not staying! If you want to wait for Daddy to come back you can do it alone, but I'm packing my stuff! *(He begins throwing whatever is left of his clothing into the duffle bag. JOAN sits on his bed.)* I'm packing it all up!

(The phone rings.)

DAVID. Go ahead, answer it. It's Daddy. Tell him what you're going to do. Tell him all the plans you have for the house. Tell him how you're going to wait for him ... Go ahead, tell him! And by the time you're finished talking, I'll be finished packing ... What are you waiting for?! *(answering the phone)* Hello ... Yeah, she's here. She can't wait to talk to you. *(DAVID hands the phone to JOAN. She holds it as he goes back to the duffle bag and slowly begins folding a shirt. She watches him then looks down at the receiver. She hangs it up. DAVID freezes for a moment and then puts the shirt into the bag as JOAN slowly leaves the room. She walks up the hallway and into her room. The two stand motionless as lights fade to black.)*

PROPERTY LIST

DAVID'S ROOM

Telephone
Radio/cassette player
Baseball bat
Baseball glove
Tennis racket
Stuffed rabbit
Record albums
Assorted games
Duffle bag
3 pornographic magazines
3 books (as indicated in script)
Cartons and crates
Clothing for packing
- Pants/jeans
- Shirts
- Shoes
- Socks

JOAN'S ROOM

Telephone
Standing picture of Daddy
Photo album
Loose photograph of Joan
Empty packet of birth control pills
Emerald green dress (with slit)
Brassiere
Cartons (also for Joan's entrance)
Suitcase

Clothing for packing
- Sweaters
- Blouses
- Skirts
- Dresses

COSTUMES

DAVID is dressed in old jeans, a short sleeve shirt, and sneakers.

JOAN wears matching sweat pants and shirt (something easy to change out of for the scene with the emerald green dress). She might also have a scarf wrapped around her hair.

* * *

Note: The props listed above are only those essential to the action of the play. Other props can be added to increase the clutter of the rooms, and give a stronger sense of the characters' past lives in the house. Very few set pieces are actually needed. Furniture and props can be placed in such a way as to suggest walls and doorways.

In DAVID'S room there is a single bed upstage, a chair (or crate) down left, and a table (or crate) down right on which the radio is placed

In JOAN'S room there is a double bed and night table upstage, a standing mirror frame down right, and a stool just upstage of the mirror. If no mirror is available the actress can mime facing the audience or side wall.

The hallway can be indicated simply by placing a long rug between the two rooms.

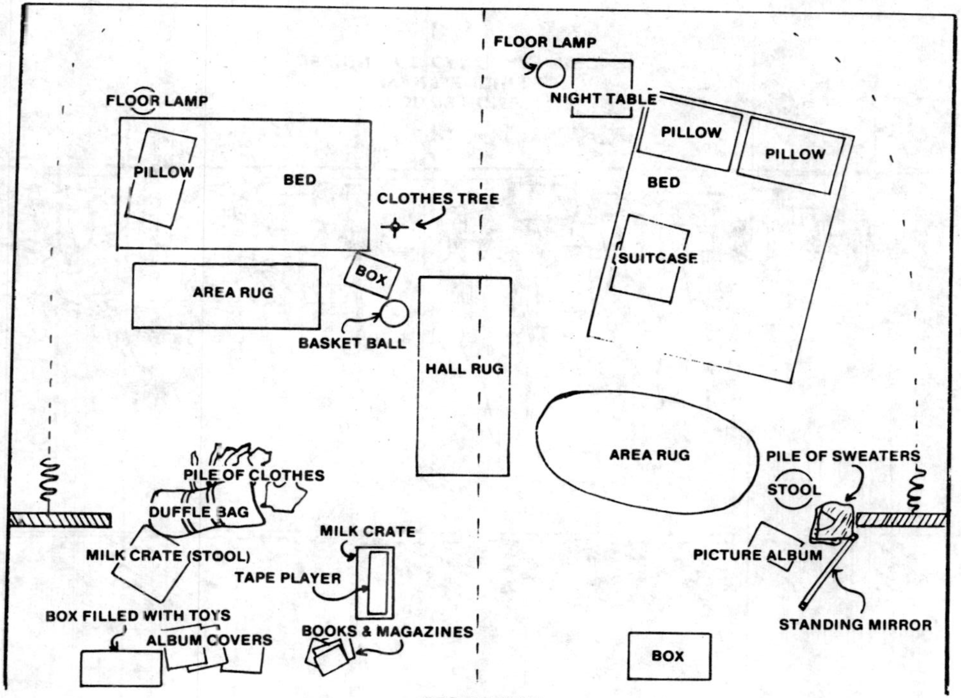

GROUND PLAN
DADDY'S HOME

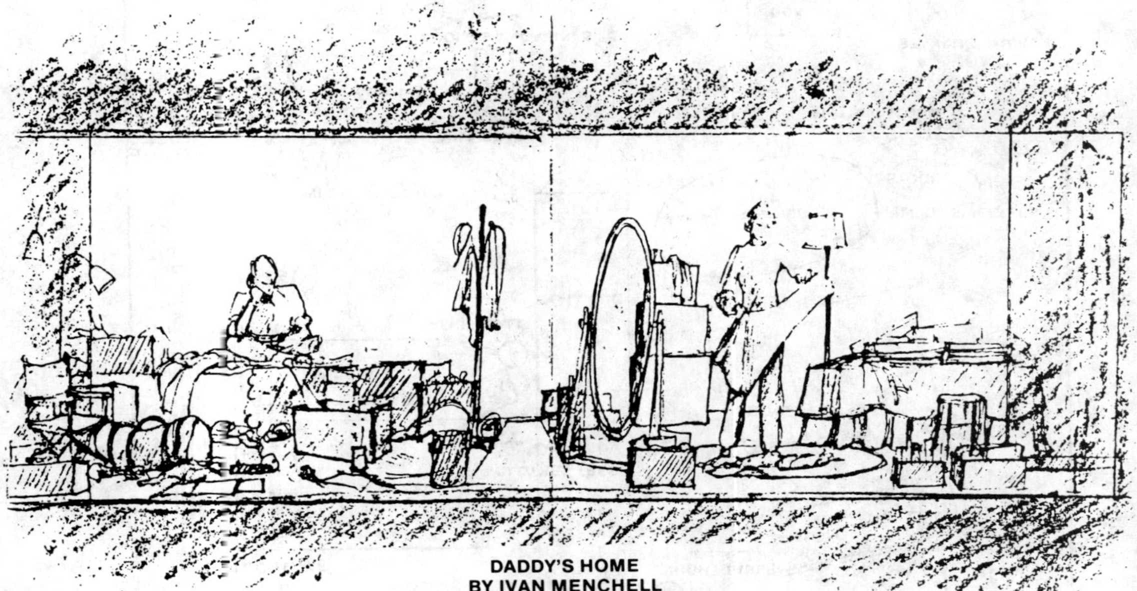

DADDY'S HOME
BY IVAN MENCHELL
DESIGN BY T. CANTU NAVARRO

RECENSIO:
a light and dark show

by
Eddie De Santis

For Patrick

RECENSIO: a light and dark show was presented in the Double Image 11th Annual Off-Off Broadway Original Short Play Festival at the Nat Horne Theatre, New York City, on May 2 and 4, 1986. It was directed by Gloria Maddox, and the production coordinator was Robert Strickstein. The cast was as follows (in order of appearance):

Sammy Pierce. . . . . Jock MacDonald

Jenny Jeffries/Patricia . . . . Sarah Burke

The characters are Sammy Pierce and Jenny Jeffries. Their ages change throughout the play. There are three basic age groups which they portray: adolescence (13, 14), young adulthood (20, 21) and adulthood (31, 32). Occasionally, Jenny will play the character of Patricia, who is about ten years old. So, as to keep the flow of the piece moving, distinct age changes and character changes are indicated by light changes, and where possible and appropriate, sound changes. The set consists basically of two chairs, moveable by the actors for scene and locale changes. Props are not needed. The actors may mime the use of various objects during the play.

Recensio is a Latin word meaning review.

RECENSIO:
a light and dark show

As the lights come up, we see JENNY preparing to draw in her sketchbook a picture of SAMMY. She is showing him how she wants him to pose with a baseball bat in his hand. He is a difficult subject. SAMMY is around thirteen. JENNY is a year older.

SAMMY. My butt hurts.

JENNY. Tough.

SAMMY. Jenny?

JENNY. I said tough. Eighth graders are big babies. You said, if I helped you build that stupid thing in the woods, that hut, you'd pose. I did and you better.

SAMMY. No. I need to ask you something. Something I'm not sure about.

JENNY. Okay. Go ahead.

SAMMY. Well, I think it's kinda personal.

JENNY. Oh. Well, if it's about these again, you can just— *(She refers to her breasts.)*

SAMMY. No, it's not about those. I don't care about those. See, today we had question and answer time in science class. Well, you know, I kinda hate it, cos Big Lips Ziegler looks so stupid standin' there and talkin' about all this stuff, cos, you know, it usually ends up being about sex questions and stuff. Like we write down questions on a piece of paper and Ziegler reads them aloud and then he tells the answer to them. But it always turns into this real kinda tellin' jokes thing. And today, well, he comes to my question and reads it. I couldn't believe it. All the girls kinda scream, you know, and groan like! Then everybody wants to know who asks it, cos they're all kinda curious to know, especially Ricky Perrine, cos he had that look on his face that if he finds out, he'll stop me in the hall and make fun of me and say stuff like "blow me" and "eat me", and I really hate it when I see him doin' it to other kids, you know. I mean, he should probably be a senior by now, but they keep holdin' him back. There's this one kid he calls worm, and...

JENNY. You mean, Worm Cunningham?

SAMMY. Yeah, him. Only you shouldn't really call him that, cos, I mean, how would you like it if somebody called you that twenty-four hours a day and kept putting glue in your hair.

JENNY. Well, he is a big fat worm. He has zits on top of zits and hairs growing out of 'em. Yucky. And he's gonna be a big fat worm when he grows up.

SAMMY. Well, I don't wanna be one, but I feel like one now. All the girls are sayin' it's such a queer question. I pretended I didn't know who asked it. I figure it must be somethin' real personal. And the bell rings and I never get my answer.

JENNY. Okay. Jeez. Just tell me the question

SAMMY. What is ... but if you tell anybody ... a period. What is a period?

JENNY. Oh, God, yuk, Sammy, I can't believe you asked that in class. That is the queerest question.

SAMMY. Why?

JENNY. Oh, you do too know.

SAMMY. I do not.

JENNY. Uh-huh.

SAMMY. Unh-uh.

JENNY. Sammy, all the boys know what that is, or at least they should know by now. Ricky Perrine knows. He knows all about periods. He came into the girls lav one day and saw the Kotex machine and started putting all these dimes in and pulling them out. It was so gross, but Connie Bennett said leave him alone, he has a lot of energy. They're goin' steady, so everything her little Ricky does is perfect. Except you know what I heard? Connie and Sara Barlow got into this real big fight in Mrs. Greenberg's French class, all cos one day Sara came into class early and she wrote on the board that the only reason Connie takes French class is cos she wants to put her tongue in all the boy's mouths, and, you know, like french them all, and they both got suspended.

SAMMY. Oh, I get it. So that's what that means.

JENNY. What?

SAMMY. French. Like with tongues and stuff.

JENNY. Of course. What'd you think, dummy?

SAMMY. My butt hurts.

JENNY. All right. Do the one with the glove. *(SAMMY gets into a pitching position.)* I'll bet you don't know what sixty-nine is either. *(silence)* Do you?

SAMMY. Sure. I know. Kind of.

JENNY. You do not.

SAMMY. I do so.

JENNY. Well, then tell me.

SAMMY. Well, maybe what you think it is, is something different than what I think it is. Let's compare.

JENNY. Okay. You first.

SAMMY. Nuh-uh. Aren't you always sayin' girls first?

JENNY. You don't even know. Eighth graders should just "fermez la bouche" anyhow. *(pause)* I'll just tell you what the six means.

SAMMY. Go ahead, tell me. I already know.

JENNY. Well. It means ... six minutes.

SAMMY. Oh, so see, ours does mean the same thing. Six minutes.

JENNY. Sure. Then what does the nine mean?

SAMMY. I'm not gonna tell you. You mean, you don't know? *(He falls out of the position.)*

JENNY. Yessir. I know. And get back into position. *(He does.)* I know. More than you did about the six minutes part, that's for sure. It's like ... nine ...

SAMMY. Yeah ...

JENNY. ... months ... and like, the one thing leads to the other ... like ...

SAMMY. Right. Like six minutes ...

JENNY. Six minutes of pleasure ... like Sister Mary William Carmelina says, that like a few moments of pleasure ... in this case, six minutes ... of pleasure can lead to ...

SAMMY. Leads to ...

JENNY. ... like nine months of pregnancy and a baby.

SAMMY. Wow. Six minutes leads to nine months. That's cool.

JENNY. Ricky Perrine writes sixty-nine everywhere. His locker is covered in 'em.

SAMMY. I'll bet I do know something you don't know.

JENNY. Sure. Like what?

SAMMY. I'll bet you don't know what queers use.

JENNY. What do you mean?

SAMMY. When they, you know, do it.

JENNY. Do what?

SAMMY. Well, you know, when the butch guy puts his thing in the femme guy ...

JENNY. *(She howls.)* What is that?

SAMMY. *(He gets out of his pitching position.)* Well, you know, one guy plays the girl, and one guy plays the guy. I don't know, that's what I heard my brother say.

JENNY. Oh, like feminine ...

SAMMY. My brother knows two of 'em. Where he works. They pack bags with him. The IGA. These two guys. And they even asked my brother if he wanted to.

JENNY. *(She howls.)* With queers? What?

SAMMY. Well, like, one of the guys ... puts ... you know ... in the other guy's ...

JENNY. *(She tries to visulize it.)* Wow. Oh. Gosh. I didn't know that.

SAMMY. So, you know what they use?

JENNY. Okay. No. I don't. Tell me.

SAMMY. Well, I heard my brother tell Jimmy Suchecki that they have to use gasoline.

JENNY. Gasoline? In their butts? How come?

SAMMY. I don't know. That's what he said. They better never light matches around there. Know what else? He said sometimes they just put their things in each other's mouth. At the same time!

JENNY. *(Her mouth drops open.)* You are kidding.

SAMMY. Pretty disgusto, right?

JENNY. No shit, Sherlock. *(She puts her hand over her mouth and laughs embarrassed.)*

SAMMY. Yeah. No shit. Fuck, fuck, fuck. *(They both start laughing wildly.)*

JENNY. Sammy Pierce, you have a dirty mouth. Fuck, shit, damn.

SAMMY. Oh, fuck you.

JENNY. *(Her laughter dies out.)* Don't say that to me. That's not funny.

SAMMY. Oh, big deal. Big "Miss Sensitive".

JENNY. Yeah, well, at least I know what periods are.

SAMMY. How'm I supposed to know?

JENNY. Doesn't your mother, you know?

SAMMY. No.

JENNY. No what? She doesn't? Or you don't know?

SAMMY. I don't know.

JENNY. God, Sammy, you are touched. Doesn't she bring home Kotex or anything like that?

SAMMY. What the hell is this Kotex stuff?

JENNY. It's for periods.

SAMMY. For periods of what?

JENNY. For period periods. For ... menstrual flow ... periods ... oh, Sammy, God. You can't just talk about periods like that. In public. In public in science class, especially. Michelle Karrenbauer is in that class and if she finds out you asked that question, she'll pass it all over school and then everybody will think you are a worm.

SAMMY. I think girls make me sick. Just tell me!

JENNY. Well, at least we don't go running around the

hall goin' blow me and eat me and stuff.

SAMMY. I know girls make me sick.

JENNY. Liar. Is that why you're always looking up my dress?

SAMMY. Yeah, sure. I wanna look up your dress and see your vagina. *(He says "vagina" with a hard "g".)*

JENNY. You don't even know what that is. You sure don't say it right. You are so touched.

(Light change on SAMMY. Young adulthood.)

SAMMY. You lean on me too much.

JENNY. I don't know why I let a mere eighth grader hang around me anyhow.

SAMMY. You're always looking over my shoulder.

(Light change on JENNY. Young adulthood. They are in the school library at college.)

JENNY. It's because I care. I want to protect what we have.

SAMMY. I feel ... stifled.

JENNY. Oh, excuse me.

SAMMY. Well, what's wrong?

JENNY. I get nervous, that's all. About graduating a year earlier.

SAMMY. What do you think's gonna happen?

JENNY. Who knows! You streaked across campus! You took your clothes off and you ran around the campus! It's like this stranger all of a sudden!

SAMMY. Oh, big deal. I say be mature about the

year apart.

JENNY. Easy for you to say.

SAMMY. You don't trust me.

JENNY. The entire world saw you. Naked. Bouncing around all over the place.

SAMMY. I asked you to come with me.

(Lights change. Adolescents.)

JENNY. Fermez la bouche, you little queer.

SAMMY. Sure, I'm queer, and you have a bush down there.

JENNY. Sammy!

SAMMY. Yeah. And I heard somebody say it's called fur pie.

JENNY. *(She wails.)* I'm tellin'.

SAMMY. Who? I'll just tell that you say "fuck" all the time.

JENNY. You're a fruit, Sammy Pierce.

SAMMY. Yeah? And how come your tits are like pencil erasers? And this picture of me stinks. You can't draw.

JENNY. *(She slaps him.)* I hate you.

SAMMY. I'm sorry, Jenny.

JENNY. Liar.

SAMMY. But I am.

JENNY. You are not. You always say stupid things. And that hurt my feelings.

SAMMY. I said I was sorry.

(Lights change. Young adulthood. SAMMY'S room in the frater-

nity house.)

SAMMY. I know what you really have a bug about.

JENNY. Nosir.

SAMMY. Yessir. The pin. The stupid pin. *(A beat.)* I give you this pin, okay? You put it on your sweater, on your blouse, wherever, then one of your sorority sisters finds out about it. And pretty soon, with all the wagging mouths chatterin' away in the libe, when they're supposed to be studyin', word gets out. Pretty soon, some little scrog queen or one of the other pinmates goes and squawks to one of the bros, and then at dinner, after everybody's finished eatin', Bergey stands up and tells everybody that the Pierceman is pinned. And then the fraternal fun begins. I get ganged up on by about fifty guys. And it's silly to struggle, because no one has ever gotten away ... ever. Soon, I find myself bound to that tree down there on High Street with a rope two inches thick, in nothin' but my underwear, cars whizzing by and everybody goin' back and forth to the libe, laughin' their buns off. But the real fun begins when I have things being flung at me, the nature of which I don't even like to think about, and the only person who can free me, of course, is you. And someone is trying, although not very hard, to find you. And God knows, you're probably in some class somewhere or at the library or uptown having one of your sorority beer blasts, while I'm standin' there covered in eggs and maple syrup and God knows what garbage, bein' humiliated in front of the whole campus. That's why I'm not givin' you my pin. Why would you want it anyhow?

JENNY. I saw it on TV, and I thought it might be fun.

SAMMY. Har de har har.

JENNY. Did you get the room for the party yet?

SAMMY. No. *(She sighs heavily.)* Okay, okay, I'll get the room for the party. Did you get the after-party party favor?

JENNY. No.

SAMMY. Jenny, I'm sick of using a raincoat. You said you'd take care of it.

JENNY. I will. God. You said we could get the room, and I want it. It'll be fun. A lot of the other brothers have already reserved one.

SAMMY. How do you know so much?

JENNY. I hear.

SAMMY. You hear?

JENNY. I won't stay here again and have somebody sleeping right there below us on the couch having sex.

SAMMY. They weren't having sex.

JENNY. Sounded pretty explicit to me.

SAMMY. You like sleepin' in the loft.

JENNY. You like sleeping in the loft. I feel spiders when I'm up there.

SAMMY. There aren't spiders.

JENNY. There are. Black ones. Hairy. I feel them.

SAMMY. I think I just read about something like that in here. Something to do with paranoid schizophrenia.

JENNY. You just sleep through it. You sleep through a lot lately.

SAMMY. Finals.

JENNY. I graduate. Two weeks. Can't believe it.

SAMMY. Yeah.

JENNY. Will you miss me?

SAMMY. Hate that question.

JENNY. Sorry. It's the last party. Just call them up and make a reservation. The Blue Ridge fills up so fast. Please, Sam, let's not sleep up there again.

SAMMY. Why are you so negative?

(Lights change. Adulthood. JENNY'S apartment in New York City.)

JENNY. I am not negative.

SAMMY. Bull. You are. This city. That's what does it. To everybody. I've seen it before. You all have this ... little itch ... that never gets scratched. This attitude. Like you're some kind of a special, chosen people. And everybody's some kind of star, competing with each other. Running around, "Do I look cool enough?", "Is my butt on straight?" Like you have to prove something. Scurrying importantly ... to nowhere. You people. Anything that happens across that river is like foreign and stupid and not good enough. You forget. I know you, Jenny. Underneath all this big apple routine. By the way, this is a great view of the river. How'd you swing that?

JENNY. Oh, so you've been bitten by the bug after all.

SAMMY. You kidding? I hate New York. While I was out with Patty today, I probably saw about five guys, taxi drivers, bums, regular people, just pull it out on the street and take a leak. Total culture shock. The sidewalks have these little yellow streams coming from the corners of buildings. I had to steer her clear of all these exhibitionists.

JENNY. You don't need to protect Patricia. She's a tough cookie. She has sense.

SAMMY. Sounds like you approve of her knowing about that kind of stuff.

-JENNY. What? People pee on the streets. I don't tell them to. Besides, it's only men. You never see any women doing it. You're the negative one. Why're you here anyhow?

(Lights change. Young adulthood. SAMMY'S room.)

SAMMY. We're like this really bad vaudeville act. And nobody's laughing.

JENNY. What?

SAMMY. It's true. We've been together for too long.

JENNY. I'm sorry. I didn't know I was such a misery to you.

(Lights change. Adulthood. JENNY'S apartment.)

JENNY. Men are such babies. I'm not trying to prove anything to anybody. I don't need to. Men see a woman in a position higher than them, and they start whining and throwing up all over the place. Their balls start shrivelling up. Well, let me tell you something, buddy. You make it here, you need a set of iron balls.

SAMMY. I wondered what I heard clanking around down there. You kill me. How urban witty. You. Everything around you. Really.

JENNY. I can see me now, still in that dumpy little apartment above the Isaly's on Maple Avenue. You'd have liked that, right? Just because you wouldn't take a little responsibility.

SAMMY. Ah, yes. The responsibility argument.

JENNY. Who's arguing? So you met her. After all this time. Do you like her?

SAMMY. What's not to like. She's smart, she's witty. Together? Huh? She seems together.

JENNY. Can it be? A soft spot?

SAMMY. I have a lot of soft spots. You just forget.

JENNY. Mmmmmm. How's what's her name? That little Italian girl ...

SAMMY. Denise ...

JENNY. Oh, yes, Denise. Her father owned all those little bakeries, didn't he?

SAMMY. How do you know so much?

JENNY. I hear.

SAMMY. You hear?

JENNY. Is she good in bed?

SAMMY. What a question.

JENNY. So, is she?

SAMMY. After she's had one or two. Like not too personal. Do you have sex?

JENNY. You mean, right now? Do I have some lying around the apartment somewhere? Let's just say, I'm satisfied.

(Lights change. Adolescents. SAMMY begins playing roughly with JENNY and tackles her.)

JENNY. I can't play green beret with you anymore, Sammy. My mom said. We can't do any of that kinda stuff anymore.

SAMMY. I want it back then.

JENNY. What?

SAMMY. My initial ring. My mom keeps lookin' in my drawers and stuff cos she doesn't see it on my hand anytime and like I made a big deal out of gettin' it for my birthday, and now she wants to know where it is. I can't tell her I just went and gave it to you.

JENNY. But you said.

SAMMY. Well.

(Lights change. Young adulthood. SAMMY and JENNY pass each other on the campus.)

JENNY. Did you get the room for the party?

SAMMY. No. D'you get the stuff?

JENNY. Don't disappoint me.

(Lights change. Adolescents.)

JENNY. We stood right down there by that creek and we threw the stones in together and you said that promise.

SAMMY. Lookey, I'll give you something if you give me the ring back.

JENNY. I don't want anything. *(pause)* What? What would you give me?

SAMMY. What do you want?

JENNY. Anything? You mean, anything I want?

SAMMY. I make like two cents at the Dairy Queen. You

have ten seconds.

JENNY. Oh, God, I can't think fast enough ...

SAMMY. Ten, nine, eight, seven ...

(Light changes on JENNY. Adulthood.)

JENNY. An estate. Anywhere. A trip around the world. A private jet to take me there. I have this thing about emeralds, tiny, not over-doing it. A Mercedes-Benz. Or a Porsche ... I can go either way on the car ...

SAMMY. ... six, five, four ...

JENNY. ... a villa overlooking the Mediterranean Sea. A duplex loft in Soho ...

SAMMY. ... three, two, one.

(Lights change on JENNY. Adolescent.)

JENNY. That new Beatle album you just got.

SAMMY. It's yours.

(Lights change. SAMMY, as an adult, with PATRICIA, a ten year old girl. They are in Central Park.)

SAMMY. Please, Patricia, take it.

PATRICIA. *(She takes what he hands her, then hands it back.)* I'm sorry. I don't want to hurt your feelings, but I don't want this. I mean, thank you. The nice idea and all. But I really am too old to play with cabbage patch dolls. Besides, I think they're pretty gross and disgusting. And a sign of the moral and ethical decline of our age.

SAMMY. Oh ... well ... I wasn't sure how you'd feel

about it. I bought a lot of accessories, too.

PATRICIA. You're not mad, are you?

SAMMY. No.

PATRICIA. Just tell them you made a mistake ... a big mistake and can you please return them. I'm sorry. Our society lets people go homeless and starve, lie wretched in the cold, damp streets, while stupid, rather unattractive dolls ... I'm sorry ... are being delivered in these fake births in these fake delivery rooms. And there is this fake doctor and this fake nurse and they walk over to these fake cabbage plants and pull out this doll. This disgusting puckered faced doll. And soon, they're giving these fake adoption papers to this nice, little kid.

SAMMY. Where do you learn these things? From your mother?

PATRICIA. Some of it. I just think it's stupid, that's all. I hate it.

SAMMY. Well, what do you like?

PATRICIA. Mmmmm, I like Billy Idol. He's real nice.

SAMMY. Thank God. *(pats her on the head)* Do you like living here?

PATRICIA. Mmmmmm, of course. *(pause)* I'm in therapy. Did you know that?

SAMMY. No. You seem a bit young for that sort of thing.

PATRICIA. I was doing bad in school. Something about not working up to my potential. He's a child psychologist. He's nice. I only see him once a week now. For a while I had to go twice. It's not a big deal anymore. A couple of my friends go to one, too.

SAMMY. Does your mother blame me?

(Lights change. Adulthood. JENNY'S apartment.)

JENNY. Of course I blame you. But only when I'm mad. Only when I'm depressed. Only when I don't have anyone else to lash out on. But if you think I sit around and pine and whine and swoon my little heart out, thinking about you, then I'm sorry to disappoint you.

SAMMY. Of course I don't think that. It's just the idea. Sending her to a shrink.

JENNY. I really think, Samuel, you don't know the first thing about it.

SAMMY. Oh, really, Jennifer? You have this edge I've never seen before.

JENNY. *(She laughs.)* It's life.

SAMMY. No. Really. You have this attitude about money and material objects.

JENNY. Why? Because I have a nice apartment? Because I don't walk around in tatters? Or is it because I have a job in the art department of one of the biggest and best advertising agencies in the city? Which pays more than minimum wage. A lot more, I might add.

SAMMY. Well, la de da.

JENNY. Yeah, well. Tough. I'm allowed. Privilege of achievement. *(He makes a face.)* I'm proud of where I am.

SAMMY. She has those kinds of attitudes, too.

JENNY. What's wrong? Doesn't Patricia act stupid enough? They do have schools, I hear, where she can have her head pumped with air. A vegetable mind, you'd probably like that better.

SAMMY. You're missing the point. She can't possibly

have any kind of a normal childhood here.

JENNY. Normal?

SAMMY. She thinks everything is ... nice.

JENNY. How nice. And what is this she? She?

SAMMY. Patricia. Okay? There. Patricia.

(Lights change. SAMMY and PATRICIA are standing at a street corner, hailing a cab.)

PATRICIA. Did she ask you what you wanted for a name?

SAMMY. Uh, no. That wouldn't have really been appropriate at the time. It's a good name, though. I like it. I like you.

PATRICIA. Oh. Can you ever come here and live?

SAMMY. No.

PATRICIA. It's a jungle, you know. But ... it's nice.

SAMMY. Yes. You could come and stay with me some time, you know. I live right outside of Cincinnati, and that's a pretty nice city. It's not as big and exciting and ... well ... as New York, but it's okay.

PATRICIA. I think I'd be too nervous.

SAMMY. Sure. I understand.

PATRICIA. I could stay with Grandma and Grandpa Jeffries, though. And visit you while I'm there. They're real nice.

SAMMY. Well, you think about it.

(Lights change. Adulthood. JENNY'S apartment.)

SAMMY. Just think about it, the things you believe in.

JENNY. I have thought about it. Long enough. Nothing. Everything. I don't know. You coming here. The fact that she's yours. The way the streets are. They way the world is. All of it. I feel good. I have love. Good friends. Patricia.

SAMMY. But there are no men around, I see. And I hear no mention of them from Patricia.

JENNY. You don't see any, that's all. And Patricia is tactful.

SAMMY. No men at all in your life? Nobody good enough?

JENNY. Oh, woe is the world of women, without men.

SAMMY. Just tell me.

JENNY. I think the saying is that behind every successful man there's a good woman, not vice versa.

SAMMY. Spout that shit to me. Maybe you're a dyke.

JENNY. I am. Is that what you need?

SAMMY. You aren't.

JENNY. So what if I was.

SAMMY. It's not ...

JENNY. No, of course, it's not. What do you want from me?

(Lights change. Young adulthood. It is summer, and they are down by the creek.)

SAMMY. Jenny, really think hard about this.

JENNY. I have. You probably think I did it on purpose. I didn't. It was that night. The party. I'm pretty sure. I heard this voice in my head. "I'm taking a chance. I'm taking a risk. Sam will kill me." I didn't do it on purpose. I just didn't care. Now I do.

(Lights change. Young adulthood. SAMMY'S room in the fraternity house.)

SAMMY. D'you get the stuff for after the party?

JENNY. I will. I just haven't had a chance.

SAMMY. Two days left. Not much time.

(Lights change. Young adulthood. Down by the creek.)

SAMMY. For Christ sakes, you are not killing anything. *(pause)* I go back to school four weeks from today. One month.

JENNY. I heard you the first time.

SAMMY. I say we go to Cincinnati, get it over with.

JENNY. No.

SAMMY. There's something wrong with this picture. Can you guess what?

JENNY. Oh, pardon me, I thought you were someone else. I've been mistaking you for someone else all along. Really, sorry about that.

SAMMY. This is insane. Why would you want to ruin my ... I mean, your life. I mean ... your life.

JENNY. My life? Your life? ITS LIFE? LIFE?

SAMMY. SHUT UP! Oh, Christ. Can't you see? It's no big deal anymore. You just have it done. And forget about it. *(pause)* What are you gonna do? How're you gonna live?

JENNY. LIVE? *(She shrugs her shoulders.)* I leave for New

York next week. I'll stay with my sister. She's gonna help.

SAMMY. OKAY! GO! I DON'T CARE! Oh, what am I saying? I can't ...

(Lights change. SAMMY as an adult and PATRICIA. Back in JENNY'S apartment after their afternoon out together.)

SAMMY. Just think about it. I'll take you horseback riding at a place nearby. These great stables.

PATRICIA. Okay. I will. Thanks for coming. I loved the show. It must have been expensive.

SAMMY. Nah. It was nothing.

PATRICIA. When you come next time, we'll go to the top of the World Trade Center. You see everything from there. When it's not windy they let you go outside. Kids my age and everything. It's real nice.

SAMMY. And we'll take the boat ride around New York.

PATRICIA. Sure. And I can show you where my friend's houseboat is.

SAMMY. Well, I wish you would write to me.

PATRICIA. No kidding? Okay. Will you write me letters back?

SAMMY. I will. Probably more post cards, though. But sure. *(He puts his coat on.)*

PATRICIA. What's that thing?

SAMMY. What?

PATRICIA. That thing that keeps shining. Inside your coat.

SAMMY. *(He mimes the following.)* Oh. This. Well ... oh,

boy ... see, you weren't really supposed to see that. But this, well, this is my pin. My ... uh ... fraternity pin. Know what that is?

PATRICIA. Sure. The one you wouldn't give Mom.

SAMMY. Right. That one. See, I wore it here for, like, good luck. You know? Like everybody needs something every once in a while for good luck. You know. I keep this, cos ... uh ... I felt really good then. I mean, not that I feel bad now, but ... you know. That was good times.

PATRICIA. Can I see it?

SAMMY. Sure. Here. God, it's a little hard to unpin. Would you do it?

PATRICIA. Sure. *(She does.)* It's real nice.

SAMMY. Thanks. See, that's the fraternity ... like ... you know, motto.

PATRICIA. What's it mean?

SAMMY. It's Latin. It means ... well, you know, I'm not really supposed to tell anybody, cos it's a big fraternity secret. It has a special handshake and everything to go with it. But I guess I can tell you. It means ... uh ... friendship forever.

PATRICIA. Oh. That is real nice. *(She hands it back. There is a long pause. He mimes putting the pin underneath the collar of her blouse. They look at each other.)*

SAMMY. But you can't ever tell anybody what the motto means. And I'll show you the secret handshake, but I'm the only one that you can do it with.

PATRICIA. Wow. Neat. Can I show Mom?

SAMMY. No. Probably not. *(pause)* Okay, sure. If you want. You decide.

PATRICIA. I'm sorry I don't call you Dad.

SAMMY. That's okay. It'd probably just make me feel old anyhow.

PATRICIA. Are you gonna show me the handshake?

SAMMY. Sure. *(He shows her the handshake.)* Then while we're shaking hands, one of us says "friendship" and the other one says "forever". *(She laughs.)* I know. It's pretty tacky. But I like it.

PATRICIA. Me too. *(She extends her hand.)* Friendship.

SAMMY. Forever.

(Lights change. Young adulthood. Down by the creek.)

JENNY. Sammy?

SAMMY. Yeah?

JENNY. I'm late.

SAMMY. What do you mean, you're late?

JENNY. I don't have my period.

SAMMY. Should you?

JENNY. Yeah. A month ago.

SAMMY. A month ago? Well, does that mean you're pregnant?

JENNY. I don't know.

SAMMY. So. What are you saying?

JENNY. I'm saying I'm late. I don't have my period. And I'm probably pregnant.

SAMMY. Oh.

JENNY. Yeah.

SAMMY. Wow.

JENNY. Yeah.

SAMMY. That is so ...

JENNY. Yeah.

SAMMY. And you're gonna have ... ?

JENNY. Mmmmm. *(She shrugs her shoulders.)*

SAMMY. Yeah. God.

JENNY. Yeah.

(Lights change. Adolescents.)

JENNY. You mean, you made out with her?

SAMMY. Yeah. So what?

JENNY. Didn't her braces cut your mouth?

SAMMY. No. You're just jealous. Look, we just frenched a little. You know.

JENNY. Was it fun?

SAMMY. Yeah. What do you think? *(long pause)* I didn't french with Susan Jones.

JENNY. You didn't?

SAMMY. We didn't even kiss. She had a piece of tuna fish ...

JENNY. What?

SAMMY. Caught in her braces. It was gross. *(JENNY laughs.)* It's not funny. I swear, if you say anything.

JENNY. I'm not gonna say anything.

SAMMY. I think about it a lot, though.

JENNY. What?

SAMMY. Kissing.

JENNY. You do?

SAMMY. Mmmmm-hhhhh. Do you?

JENNY. Mmmm. Sometimes. *(pause)* Constantly.

SAMMY. Oh, yeah?

JENNY. Yeah. *(long pause)* We could try it if you wanna.

SAMMY. Really?

JENNY. Uh-huh. We just each have to promise that if we don't like it, we just say so and stop. And the other person's feelings won't be hurt.

SAMMY. You think of everything.

JENNY. Of course. Is that a promise?

SAMMY. Okay.

JENNY. Come sit here. *(He sits close to her. What follows is a tender love scene between two adolescents for the first time. They kiss each other at first probingly, embarrassed, then deeply. They take a moment to let it all sink in. Soon, they become very passionate. SAMMY kisses JENNY over her face, her neck and moves to the top of her blouse and finally kisses her breasts.)*

SAMMY. Oh, Jenny. Oh, God, I'm gonna go crazy.

JENNY. You kiss real good.

SAMMY. You do, too. Do you think maybe we should ... this is like we should be dating?

JENNY. I don't know. *(They sit there, embarrassed for a moment.)*

SAMMY. I'm glad we're friends. I mean, at least we know each other and ... well, you know.

JENNY. *(She hugs him.)* Oh, Sammy.

(The lights go down, except on their faces. SAMMY'S face is most visible to the audience, and just for a moment a cloud passes over it, then moves on. Lights go down.)

— END OF PLAY —

THE TIES THAT BIND
by
Matthew Witten

MATTHEW WITTEN has had several plays produced in Boston, including ALASKA FIRE, WELCOME TO PLANET EARTH, THE BODY PARTS, A HELL OF A HEAVENLY TIME, LIFELINES, and SLOW LEAK. THE TIES THAT BIND is his third play to be produced in New York, and his work has also been presented in Los Angeles, San Francisco, Atlanta, Virginia Beach, Roanoke, and Ashland, Oregon. He has coproduced new play festivals in Boston for Playwrights' Platform and Touchstone Productions, and has received playwriting grants from the Massachusetts Artists Foundation, the Massachusetts Arts Lottery Council, and the New England Foundation for the Arts.

THE TIES THAT BIND had its first New York production at the Quaigh Theatre on January 1, 1986, directed by Brian Delate with the following cast:

DAVID .... Mark Shannon

EILEEN......................... Nancy Stewart Hill

SANDY .... Dani Klein

The play was produced by the Quaigh Theatre and the Off-Off Broadway Short Play Festival from April 28 to May 9, 1986, directed by Scott Kanoff with the following cast:

DAVID.................................. Ken Myles

EILEEN......................... Nancy Stewart Hill

SANDY .... Dani Klein

CAST OF CHARACTERS

DAVID
SANDY
EILEEN

All three characters are in their thirties.

SET

The nicely furnished living room of a condo.

TIME

Late evening, the present.

THE TIES THAT BIND

LIGHTS UP! A nicely furnished living room. Laughter offstage. SANDY and DAVID enter stage right, laughing. She drops her key, they laugh, and he looks around the room.

DAVID. Nice place.
SANDY. Thank you. Hey Eileen!
DAVID. Who's Eileen?
SANDY. She's my friend that's visiting. I want you to meet her. *(They embrace and kiss.)*
DAVID. You know, this is incredible.
SANDY. What do you mean?
DAVID. We meet in a bar ... Two strangers ... We start talking, it's like we've known each other all our lives. Couple hours later I'm in your home ... I meet your friends ...

(EILEEN enters.)

EILEEN. Hi.
SANDY. This is David.
DAVID. Hi, Eileen.
EILEEN. Hi. Would you like some coffee?
SANDY. I wouldn't mind some coffee.
EILEEN. It's no trouble. I already made a pot.
DAVID. Okay.
EILEEN. I'll heat it up. *(She exits into the kitchen.)*
DAVID. How come she made a pot of coffee so late at

night? Was she waiting up for you?

SANDY. No. She likes to have coffee ready in the morning.

DAVID. She was really checking me out. I had to look to make sure my clothes were still on.

SANDY. She always does that.

DAVID. What do you mean, always?

SANDY. Come on, we just met. You can't get jealous yet.

DAVID. Okay. *(takes her into a little dance and dances her over to the sofa)* Won't you sit down? *(She sits.)* Your shoulders are all hunched up.

SANDY. I keep the heat too low here. I should turn it up. *(starts to get up)*

DAVID. No, no, no. Relax. *(massages her neck and shoulders)* Are you nervous about inviting me over?

SANDY. A little bit.

DAVID. We don't have to sleep together tonight.

SANDY. No, I want to.

DAVID. Your shoulders are hunched up. *(She pushes her shoulders down, but they come up again.)* You can do it.

SANDY. I'm cold.

DAVID. *(hugs her to warm her up)* Do we really want coffee?

SANDY. I'm tired.

DAVID. Let's go to bed.

SANDY. Let's talk for awhile first.

DAVID. Sure, but with your friend here we can't really talk.

SANDY. I want you guys to talk.

DAVID. I'll talk to her next time.

SANDY. She's only in town for a couple of days.

DAVID. You know what's funny? You have this way of being aggressive and shy at the same time. I like that. I like you. You like me too, hunh?

SANDY. Yeah.

DAVID. Nothing like this has ever happened to me.

SANDY. Come on. You've picked up girls before.

DAVID. I never picked anyone up at a bar before.

SANDY. Come on. A smooth guy like you?

DAVID. This is incredible. It's almost spooky. It's been exactly one year since my wife and I got divorced. One year to the day. I haven't been with anybody since then. I haven't met anybody I wanted to be with. But now exactly a year later we meet — and this is anything but an ordinary encounter, you know what I mean? Listen to me, I'm just rambling on here. Sandy, you're something special.

(DAVID kisses her. EILEEN enters with a coffee tray. She pauses and watches them kiss, and then moves forward. SANDY and DAVID stop kissing.)

EILEEN. Excuse me.

DAVID. *(reaches out for the coffee)* Thanks. *(EILEEN looks at DAVID a bit too long. DAVID jokes:)* I feel like Older Sister is checking me out.

SANDY. Eileen is like an older sister to me.

EILEEN. So, what do you do for a living, young man?

DAVID. I sell drugs.

SANDY. He's an English professor.

DAVID. So how long are you visiting for?

SANDY. Would you like some sugar?

EILEEN. So how was The Plough and The Stars?

DAVID. It was wonderful.

EILEEN. Do you go there often?

DAVID. No, this was my first time. I'm divorced and I don't have herpes. Is there anything else you'd like to know?

EILEEN. Oh, you were married before. Do you have children?

SANDY. Eileen is a lawyer. She can't help herself. He has two children.

DAVID. I better use the bathroom before I drink this coffee.

SANDY. It's through the bedroom.

DAVID. I'll find it. *(He exits.)*

EILEEN. *(watches him go)* Look at his back.

SANDY. Why?

EILEEN. Is something wrong with it?

SANDY. Not that I noticed.

EILEEN. It seemed a little bit hunched over.

SANDY. *(irritated)* Eileen—

EILEEN. What if there's something wrong with his back?

SANDY. Eileen—

EILEEN. What?

SANDY. There's nothing wrong with his back. Every guy I bring home you find something wrong with.

EILEEN. Sandy. I like him. He's a good size. He has bright eyes.

SANDY. He's a professor, and he's smart.

EILEEN. If he does have scoliosis, it might not be a problem. But let's ask him, okay? Wouldn't you feel more secure if we ask him?

SANDY. How're we gonna ask him? I don't wanna lose this guy.

EILEEN. We'll think of a way.

SANDY. Just watch yourself. You were really making him nervous.

EILEEN. Sandy, be fair. Give me a chance to check him out. You had three hours with him at the Plough. I haven't had five minutes.

SANDY. I just wanna get this over with.

EILEEN. *(see DAVID, offstage)* Shh.

(DAVID enters.)

DAVID. Hi.

SANDY. Could I ask you to get some milk for my coffee while you're up?

DAVID. Isn't that milk there? *(points to the creamer on the coffee tray)*

SANDY. No, that's cream. I prefer milk.

DAVID. Okay, I'll get you some.

SANDY. Thanks. *(SANDY and EILEEN watch DAVID exit into the kitchen. To EILEEN, upset:)* He does have a little bit of a hunch.

EILEEN. Look. It's probably not hereditary.

SANDY. How do we find out?

EILEEN. We'll think of a way.

SANDY. I know exactly how to do it. Leave it to me.

EILEEN. What are you gonna say?

DAVID. *(calls from the kitchen, offstage:)* Can I come out yet? *(appears in the entranceway from the kitchen)* I can go to the bathroom again if you want to talk about me some more.

SANDY. Did you hear what we were saying?

DAVID. *(enters with milk)* No. What were you saying?

SANDY. I was telling Eileen how in touch you are with postures.

DAVID. I am?

SANDY. Well I mean the way you were noticing before about my shoulders being hunched up? How did you get to be so perceptive about postures? Did you study Alexander technique or polarity or something like that?

DAVID. *(shakes his head)* I have scoliosis. That's probably why I notice other people's postures.

EILEEN. Scoliosis? What's that?

DAVID. Curvature of the spine. *(turns sideways so they can see his posture)*

EILEEN. Is it hereditary?

DAVID. *(to SANDY)* Your older sister's getting a little carried away, Sandy. *(to EILEEN)* This is just our first date. We don't have to worry about that kind of thing.

EILEEN. Is it a troublesome issue for you to talk about?

DAVID. I can tell you're a good lawyer.

EILEEN. I can tell you'd be a tough witness. You can plead the fifth if you like.

DAVID. It's not hereditary in my case.

SANDY. *(sighs with relief)* You must be glad about that.

DAVID. I seem to be missing something here.

EILEEN. I'm really interested in hereditary diseases.

DAVID. Why's that? *(EILEEN tries to think of an answer.)*

SANDY. It's really boring. You don't want to hear about it.

DAVID. No, no, I'm curious.

EILEEN. I have a number of clients who are suing companies for health problems related to hazardous waste. So I've had to learn alot about hereditary diseases.

DAVID. Hunh.

EILEEN. Do you have any?

DAVID. Hayfever.

EILEEN. That's wonderful.

DAVID. Hayfever is wonderful?

EILEEN. It's wonderful that you don't have any other hereditary diseases.

DAVID. I suppose it is.

SANDY. Yes, it's wonderful. *(All three of them are giggling.)*

EILEEN. Do you have a history of cancer in your family?

DAVID. No, my family has a history of heart disease.

EILEEN. Oh, at what age?

DAVID. At what age what?

EILEEN. Oh, at what age do they — you know ... *(puts her hand across her throat in a throat-slitting gesture)*

DAVID. Sixty-five. Seventy.

SANDY. That's not so bad. That's about average.

EILEEN. Yeah, I guess it's all right.

DAVID. I'm glad you guys think so. *(They finish giggling.)*

EILEEN. The human body is a wonderful thing. Life is a

gift. I thank God every day that I've never been sick. I mean — really sick. *(to DAVID)* Have you ever been sick? I mean ... really sick?

DAVID. I had an appendectomy once. You wanna see my scar?

EILEEN. Do you know what I'd really like to see?

DAVID. I'm not sure I wanna know.

EILEEN. Do you have any pictures of your kids?

DAVID. Sandy. Your friend is really wild. *(takes out his wallet)* Yeah, I happen to have one right here. Jennifer's the big one. Susan's the little one.

SANDY. Oh, they're beautiful. You must be really proud of them. Eileen, aren't they beautiful?

EILEEN. Yes, they are. Do you have mostly girls in your family?

DAVID. I don't really know.

EILEEN. I'm being nosy. I'll go into the kitchen.

SANDY. You don't have to go.

EILEEN. It's just the kitchen. You two lovebirds have a good time now. I'm gonna bake brownies.

SANDY. Are you sure? *(EILEEN gives SANDY a smile and exits to the kitchen.)*

DAVID. You take her opinion very seriously, don't you?

SANDY. I meant was she sure she didn't mind going to the kitchen

DAVID. It's one-thirty in the morning. Is she really going to bake brownies?

SANDY. She always cooks when she's nervous.

DAVID. What does she got to be nervous about?

SANDY. I guess she feels a little awkward.

DAVID. So do I. Sandy, look, I'm feeling a little weird. I don't know if I'm up for a wild night. Let's get together this weekend.

SANDY. I want you to stay with me tonight.

DAVID. I'd like to, Sandy, I really would.

SANDY. Let's go to bed.

DAVID. I don't know. *(SANDY kisses him, and they hug.)* This is nice. But your shoulders are about a foot higher than they were before.

SANDY. I'm a little nervous.

DAVID. We don't have to rush into this.

SANDY. I want your body. *(beat)* I'm lonely. *(beat)* Don't you ever have loneliness attacks?

DAVID. But you have your friend staying here with you. *(SANDY tries to kiss him, but he pulls away.)* Why are you so eager to sleep with me tonight? And why was she asking me all those questions?

SANDY. She's funny.

DAVID. And when I was in the bathroom, I overheard you say to her, "I just want to get this over with." What was that all about? And why did she hush you up when she saw me coming?

SANDY. I was just saying, I want to get the seduction over with so we can go to bed.

DAVID. *(pause)* Is there some reason you want to sleep with me before Eileen leaves?

SANDY. That's ridiculous. Why would I want to do that?

DAVID. I don't know. Maybe she's your sex therapist.

SANDY. You really are being ridiculous.

DAVID. I *feel* ridiculous. I'm not in the habit of saying no to beautiful women. I like you very much, but ...

SANDY. You're scared of me because I'm not playing hard-to-get.

DAVID. I haven't slept with anybody in a year.

SANDY. *(pause)* I won't bite you, I promise.

DAVID. You can bite me a little bit.

SANDY. Okay, I will.

DAVID. Look, I'd like to get to know you.

SANDY. Sleeping with people is the best way to get to know them. Come on, David. We talked at the Plough for three hours.

DAVID. Sandy. Give me your phone number. I promise I'll give you a call. *(SANDY shakes her head.)* Why are you shaking your head? You won't give me your number?

SANDY. I want you tonight.

DAVID. How about this weekend? *(SANDY hangs her head.)* Can I give you my number? *(SANDY shakes her head.)* You don't want my number? *(SANDY holds out her arms to DAVID.)* Sandy ... I can't get into it. *(DAVID goes to the door.)*

SANDY. David?

DAVID. *(at the door)* Yes?

SANDY. Eileen and I want you to be the father of our child.

DAVID. *(pause)* What?

(EILEEN enters.)

SANDY. Eileen and I want you to be the father of our child.

EILEEN. What are you doing?

SANDY. *(to EILEEN)* He was walking out the door. *(to DAVID)* We're sorry we tricked you into it. We didn't know any other way to do it.

DAVID. Are you ...

EILEEN. *(nods)* I'm not really an out-of-town guest.

DAVID. Or an older sister.

SANDY. I said she was *like* an older sister.

DAVID. Do you do this every night? Get all dressed up an' ... hit the town?

SANDY. Only once a month. When I'm ovulating.

DAVID. How do you know when you're ovulating?

SANDY. My temperature goes up and my mucus changes.

DAVID. So tonight was the big night? You were sitting there at The Plough, sipping wine, asking me questions about my job, and ovulating.

EILEEN. You should feel honored that she chose you.

SANDY. You should feel honored that she approved.

EILEEN. You're the third guy Sandy brought home. I didn't approve the other two.

DAVID. Three guys in one night?!

SANDY. No, we've been doing this for five months.

EILEEN. We were a little worried about your scoliosis. We thought it might be hereditary.

SANDY. Not that it's very noticeable.

DAVID. Were you planning to ever tell me?

EILEEN. You have to look at it from our point of view.

SANDY. Eileen an' I want a child. What should we do? What would you do?

DAVID. I don't know. It's not my problem.

EILEEN. Exactly.

SANDY. David, you would never have known.

DAVID. Exactly. I would never know that I was a father.

SANDY. You wouldn't be a father. Biologically, yes, you would be. But you wouldn't be a parent.

DAVID. What seems a parent to you may not be apparent to me.

EILEEN. You would be a sperm donor. That's all. Sandy and I will be the parents. We take full responsibility.

DAVID. Thank you for offering to take care of my child. That's very kind of you.

EILEEN. Look, if you're so concerned about what happens to your sperm, you shouldn't pick up women in bars.

DAVID. "I want your body." "I'm lonely. Don't you ever have loneliness attacks?"

SANDY. I'm sorry.

DAVID. Don't apologize. I'm just suggesting if you try this again, come up with better lines. "I want your body."

SANDY. I don't have much experience at seducing men.

DAVID. Why do you have to pick up strangers in bars? Don't you have any men friends? Why can't you hit on one of them for a donation?

SANDY. David, that would be too weird.

DAVID. This isn't weird? *(beat)*

SANDY. You have to remember, this is not what Eileen an' I planned on.

DAVID. If I became a father without knowing it, that wouldn't be weird?

EILEEN. Well, maybe so, but it happens all the time.

DAVID. Not to me it doesn't.

EILEEN. Really? You pick up women for one-night stands. How do you know you're not a father already?

DAVID. I take precautions. Besides, what makes you think I pick up women for one-night stands? I haven't had one of them since college.

EILEEN. What were you planning to do with Sandy? Eat popcorn?

DAVID. Tonight was very unusual for me.

EILEEN. Right. You fell madly in love with Sandy at first sight.

DAVID. Maybe I did. Stranger things have happened.

EILEEN. Listen. We're all getting pretty irritable here. Why don't we just sit down.

DAVID. *(to SANDY)* Why did you choose me to be the father?

SANDY. You had the best sense of humor of anyone at the Plough.

DAVID. I looked like a nice funny hunk of genetic material?

SANDY. If I didn't like you, I would never have had the nerve to bring you home.

DAVID. My ex-wife is gay. I have to get out of the habit of falling in love with lesbians.

EILEEN. You're not in love with Sandy. Look. Why don't we call it a night.

DAVID. I thought you wanted my help.

SANDY. We do.

EILEEN. Sandy, come on—

SANDY. Would you do it for us?

EILEEN. It wouldn't work out, Sandy—

SANDY. Hang on a second.

DAVID. It could be my good deed for the day. Be alot more fun than helping an old lady across the street.

SANDY. You think sex with me would be fun?

DAVID. I love the way you kiss. *(to EILEEN)* If you don't mind my saying so.

EILEEN. I do mind.

SANDY. David, I'm gay.

EILEEN. It might interfere with your fun.

DAVID. Are you really gay? You're not even bisexual?

SANDY. I don't think so.

DAVID. Is that ambiguity?

SANDY. I haven't slept with a guy for five years. When I did, I didn't enjoy it.

DAVID. People do change. *(to EILEEN)* If you don't mind my saying so.

EILEEN. I do mind. *(to SANDY)* Let's quit fooling around. He's not serious.

SANDY. Are you serious?

DAVID. Sure, I'm serious. This could be my new hobby. I could be a modern-day Johnny Appleseed, spreading joy wherever I go. You're a very nice lady. *(to EILEEN)* You I'm not sure about. If you don't mind me saying so.

EILEEN. You don't make a big effort to be pleasant, do you?

DAVID. Give me something to like about you.

EILEEN. Why should I?

DAVID. Because I have the sperm.

EILEEN. I want this guy out of our apartment.

SANDY. Forget it.

DAVID. Sandy—

SANDY. Look, Eileen, we've been looking for a guy for five months.

EILEEN. So we'll look for five more.

SANDY. You're not the one who has to look.

DAVID. Why don't you go to a sperm bank?

EILEEN. Exactly.

SANDY. Hey. I want to meet the father, okay? Is that all right? Does it seem weird to you that I want to meet the father of my child? Does it seem unnatural?

EILEEN. Sandy, we made an agreement!

SANDY. I couldn't help it! He was walking out the door!

EILEEN. He would want visitation rights.

SANDY. *(to DAVID, angrily)* Would you want visitation rights?

EILEEN. I don't care what he wants. I don't like him.

SANDY. Am I ever gonna find a guy that you think is okay?

EILEEN. Yes.

SANDY. What about the last guy? What was wrong with him?

EILEEN. Give me a break. The guy was a fucking drunk.

DAVID. Does she always feel so positive about men?

SANDY. It's just the circumstances. She's jealous.

EILEEN. Don't justify me, Sandy.

SANDY. Look, if I was David, the way you're behaving, I'd have serious doubts about you myself.

EILEEN. If you were David, I wouldn't give a shit.

DAVID. Maybe I should just ... *(gets up to go)*

SANDY. *(pushes him down in his seat)* No! *(pause, quietly)* Please don't.

DAVID. I hope you guys don't fight like this very often.

SANDY. No, we don't fight like this very often.

EILEEN. It's none of your business how often we fight.

DAVID. You remind me of my ex-wife.

EILEEN. Oh, and you want to get back at her, is that it? Is that why you wanna sleep with Sandy? Hunh?

DAVID. If she's always this unpleasant around men, I don't think she should—

EILEEN. Hey. Some of my best friends are men.

SANDY. David, she does have alot of male friends. I think she'd be a good parent.

DAVID. Could she relate to the kid if it was a boy? *(pause)*

SANDY. Answer him.

EILEEN. No. He's just playing with us. He thinks I'm his ex-wife.

SANDY. It's a reasonable question. Answer it.

EILEEN. I find it offensive that he thinks because I'm gay I can't relate to boys.

SANDY. It's offensive. Okay. So what. Answer him. If

you don't at least give him a chance, I won't bring the next one home.

EILEEN. Don't threaten me.

SANDY. I'm sorry. I'm sorry. I just can't stand it. I'm never gonna have children. *(pause)* Please give this a chance.

EILEEN. *(to DAVID, quietly)* Look. When my father left, he left me to take care of my little brother alone. We're very close. He's grown now. He's married, he has a beautiful wife, and two little boys of his own. I babysit for them often. We play around together. I take them to the park. We have a good time. I love those kids, but I want kids of my own.

SANDY. Thank you, Eileen. *(pause)* We're usually not like this. It's just a hard thing for us. We've been living together for four years. We're really very stable.

DAVID. *(to SANDY)* What about you? Why do you want kids?

SANDY. I love children. I'm a teacher, and I've always wanted kids of my own. And now I have a good job and a nice condo ... and I met the person I want to spend my life with. I'm a happy adult. I'd love having a kid. I think the kid would love having me. *(beat)*

EILEEN. Would you be willing to sign a contract relinquishing all parental rights, including visitation rights?

DAVID. You really are a lawyer, aren't you? *(pause)* Is it just to please Sandy?

EILEEN. What?

DAVID. Do you want a child just because Sandy wants one?

EILEEN. No, I want one too. I want kids. You know, I

can't help resenting your questions. I know they're perfectly reasonable. But if we were straight, we could be ex-convicts with a history of child-molesting, and we wouldn't have to answer them. It would be okay. Do you think this is easy for me? Do you think I like the idea of baking brownies in the kitchen while you and Sandy are in the bedroom creating our baby? I'm not a saint.

DAVID. It takes a lot of courage.

EILEEN. It takes a deep desire to have children.

DAVID. I suspect you would be a decent parent.

EILEEN. Thank you.

DAVID. You're welcome. I suspect you'll be better than most fathers are.

EILEEN. Thank you.

DAVID. Of course that's not saying much.

SANDY. David, please don't make jokes.

DAVID. I'm serious here. I mean, this is really interesting. How often in life does a man get a chance like this? A chance to be profoundly important ... but with no responsibility. I mean, to tell the truth I've been a lousy father ever since we got divorced. It hurts. But if I do this, I can have a fantasy. The kid will grow up to be the next Albert Einstein. Or Mahatma Gandhi. Maybe one day he'll negotiate total nuclear disarmament. Maybe ... I like this. For the next forty years I can fantasize about the great kid I fathered one night, back in 1986. What the hell. If you want to do it, I'll do it.

EILEEN. Would you want visitation rights?

DAVID. No. I want a dream. If the kid fucks up in real life, I don't wanna know about it. I already have two kids to visit. It's not much fun. It's not much fun at all.

EILEEN. You don't want visitation rights. In fifteen years, you can't change your mind.

DAVID. If I donate my talent for this kid, I don't want to ever see him. I don't want him to ever know it was me. And I don't want to know your last name.

SANDY. *(to EILEEN)* If this is how he feels, if you and I and the child will never have to see him again after this evening ...

EILEEN. Let's do it.

SANDY. Thank you, Eileen.

EILEEN. Well. I guess I'll go check on those brownies. I'm gonna work on that contract. No visitation rights.

DAVID. Wouldn't it be funny if I couldn't get it up?

SANDY. No.

EILEEN. Not at all.

DAVID. Could I ask you something? If the kid is a boy, could you have someone teach him how to throw a baseball? I wouldn't want him to end up throwing like this. *(demonstrates a wrong way to throw a baseball)*

EILEEN. We'll hire a coach. *(EILEEN "slaps him five" and exits to the kitchen.)*

DAVID. Seen any good movies lately?

SANDY. We should go to the bedroom.

DAVID. Do you have any hard liquor?

SANDY. Scotch.

DAVID. Good.

SANDY. We really appreciate this, David.

DAVID. Always glad to be of service.

SANDY. Do you want some ice?

DAVID. *(shakes his head)* Don't bother with a glass. Just bring the bottle.

SANDY. Are you nervous?

DAVID. It's been a long time.

SANDY. I'm nervous too.

DAVID. When did you decide you were gay?

SANDY. Give me a break. Let's go to bed.

DAVID. I want a kiss first.

SANDY. All right.

DAVID. Lower your shoulders. *(They kiss.)*

SANDY. *(whispers)* You're very attractive.

DAVID. Why is that?

SANDY. *(whispers)* You have a very gentle kiss.

DAVID. It's not fiery and passionate?

SANDY. You try so hard to be sarcastic. But you're really a very gentle person. *(pause)* What's wrong? *(pause)* We should go to bed.

DAVID. Sandy ...

SANDY. What is it?

DAVID. I don't know. I do think you're something very special.

SANDY. David, I'm not something special.

DAVID. I don't know. I guess I believe in love at first sight.

SANDY. David, please don't be dramatic. I want a child. Please help me. *(They start heading for the bedroom, but DAVID stops.)*

DAVID. Sandy. Do you have one of those, unh, what do you call those things, unh, turkey baster?

SANDY. A turkey baster? Oh, a turkey baster. Um. No, but we do have an applicator.

DAVID. An applicator? Are we talking about the same thing?

SANDY. I bought it when we were thinking about using a sperm bank. Just to see how I felt about it.

DAVID. How did you feel about it?

SANDY. Well I decided against it, as you can see.

DAVID. How come?

SANDY. I wanted to meet the father.

DAVID. Meet him.

SANDY. Talk to him. See what he looks like.

DAVID. You didn't want to sleep with him.

SANDY. I was willing to.

DAVID. Get your applicator.

SANDY. Are you sure it's okay?

DAVID. Get your applicator. I'll start thinking private thoughts. *(Puts his jacket over his head. SANDY exits. DAVID takes out his wallet and removes the photograph of his kids. He takes the jacket off his head and looks at the photo for a few moments. SANDY enters, carrying a small bag.)*

SANDY. It's in here.

DAVID. *(takes the bag; pause)* I'll use the bedroom. This won't take long. I've been excited all night.

SANDY. Take your time.

(DAVID exits into the bedroom. SANDY stares after him for a couple of moments, then walks slowly to the couch and sits down. EILEEN enters from the kitchen, carrying a pad of paper.)

EILEEN. What's going on?

SANDY. He's using the applicator.

EILEEN. Whose idea was that?

SANDY. It was his. But I'm glad. *(giggles nervously)*

EILEEN. So am I. *(They hug.)*

SANDY. Tell me a story, Eileen.

EILEEN. Not now. I have to get cooking on this contract.

SANDY. Please? We need a story.

EILEEN. Once upon a time there was a man who — hereby waives all parental rights, including visitation rights, with respect to the child of Eileen and Sandy Pfeiffer-Hoyt.

SANDY. You're doing a lousy job of telling the story.

EILEEN. I rather like it. In the event that David — what's his last name?

SANDY. I don't know.

EILEEN. In the event that David Blank ever requests permission to contact said child, such permission shall not be granted.

SANDY. I love you, Eileen.

EILEEN. Are you scared?

SANDY. If you won't tell me a story, I better tell you one.

EILEEN. Sure.

SANDY. It's an old Russian folk tale. Actually, it's a proverb. It goes like this. Are you listening?

EILEEN. Yeah.

SANDY. If the two parents are thinking peaceful, happy thoughts at the time of conception, then the baby grows up to be peaceful and happy. So we have to think good thoughts, okay? Think good thoughts. *(They think. Beat.)*

EILEEN. I almost got one. Come on, good thought! Come on! Oh no. My brain is running into rough waters. Heretofore. Inasmuch. Whereas. Said child. Maybe you should go first.

SANDY. I wonder what David is thinking about.

EILEEN. I hope he's thinking about naked women.

SANDY. I hope he's thinking about how his children will grow up and go to college, and they won't be living with his ex-wife any more, and they'll visit him on vacations, and they'll have a really good time together, and he'll get married again, and his new wife and his kids will get along really well together, and they'll all go out and play miniature golf.

EILEEN. Why miniature golf?

SANDY. I didn't realize how hard this would be.

EILEEN. Same here.

SANDY. I don't know, Eileen.

EILEEN. What?

SANDY. I want the baby to belong to you and me. And no one else. If we have a kid by him, he'll always mean something to me.

EILEEN. Holy shit, Sandy.

SANDY. I don't know. Maybe we should have used a sperm bank.

EILEEN. That certainly was my preference.

SANDY. Don't be angry with me.

EILEEN. I'm not angry.

SANDY. All I want is one little sperm.

EILEEN. Any contact whatsoever between David Blank and said child, or between David Blank and said child's parents, shall be considered a violation of this contract.—

SANDY. What should we do, Eileen?

(EILEEN tries to think of an answer. DAVID enters, carrying the bag.)

DAVID. Pretty fast, hunh? Don't open this 'til Christmas. I'm kind of shy. *(solemnly holds up the bag)* I hereby entrust you will all the responsibilities and privileges of parenthood. May the baby grow up to be healthy, wealthy and wise.

EILEEN. Thank you.

DAVID. *(holds out the bag and slowly, solemnly walks to SANDY)* The passing of the sperm. An ancient ritual. Usually the ritual is done a little differently. *(SANDY takes the bag. To EILEEN.)* Is that the contract?

EILEEN. I still have to finish it.

DAVID. I'll sign it now. You can finish it later. *(signs it)*

EILEEN. Don't you want to read it?

DAVID. No, I trust you.

EILEEN. I'll send you a copy.

DAVID. Okay. I better be going.

EILEEN. What's your address?

DAVID. UMass/Boston. Listen, I want you to know something. I wish you both all the best and all the happiness. I really do.

SANDY. We really appreciate this, David.

EILEEN. Yes, we do.

DAVID. Good luck. *(DAVID exits.)*

SANDY. Well, we finally got it. *(walks to EILEEN, sits down)*

EILEEN. But do you want to use it?

SANDY. This is your decision too. Look, I don't wanna do this if we're not thinking happy thoughts. *(beat)* Tell me a story.

EILEEN. Sandy ...

SANDY. Come on, Eileen, we need a good one. We need to feel peaceful and happy.

EILEEN. Okay. I'll tell you the story of Eve. *(holds SANDY)* When Eve was pregnant for the first time, she said to God, "God, how should I raise my children?" And God answered, "I don't know. Look what a mess I made trying to raise you and Adam. Because of Me, you got thrown out of Paradise." So Eve got upset, and she said to God, "God, take this baby away from me. I'm not ready. I'm not smart enough. I shouldn't have eaten the apple, and Adam and I are having a lot of arguments lately, and I'm just not ready." And God answered, "Woman. You will never feel ready. You will always be afraid. Rich or poor, young or old, gay or straight, you will always be afraid. But for as long as the stars are in the sky, for as long as they shine in the heavens, you will have children."

SANDY. I like that story. Eileen, what the hell. Let's go ahead. *(EILEEN smiles and nods. SANDY looks in the bag and says.)* There it is. *(sees something else in the bag)* And here's the picture of his kids. *(takes the photo out; they look at it, then put it down)*

(EILEEN and SANDY smile at each other, stand up, and head for the bedroom. They stop; EILEEN comes back to the table and picks up the bag; and then they exit to the bedroom, as the lights fade to black.)

THE END

PROPS

SANDY
Key
Small bag

EILEEN
Coffee tray
3 cups of coffee
Sugar
Cream
Pad of paper
Pen

DAVID
Milk
Wallet
Photo of two kids

COSTUMES

SANDY wears a pretty dress, DAVID wears a tweed jacket and nice cotton slacks, and EILEEN is casually dressed for an evening at home

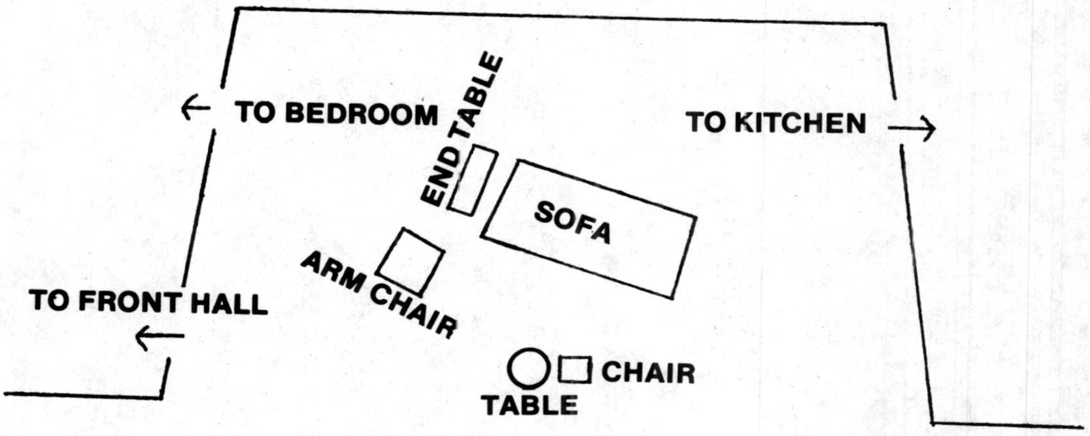

THE TIES THAT BIND
GROUND PLAN

GHOST STORIES
by
Annie Evans

GHOST STORIES was presented by Double Image Theatre, Inc. in the 11th Annual Short Play Festival under the direction of Toni Kotite, under the stage management of Blake Riley, with the following cast:

Alex . . . . Olivia Birkelund

Dodie . . . . Terry Urdang

Margaret . . . . Amanda Green

CHARACTERS

Alex Robinson — *25 years old, from first glance a pretty, well adjusted housewife, actually desperately disillusioned to the point of suicide.*

Sally "Dodie" Schmidt — *25 years old, slightly plump, eyes crying for a hug. Terrified to move away from the home of Alex, Margaret and her youth.*

Margaret Holland — *25 years old, confident and career oriented, carries the markings of higher education, noticeably over-driven.*

SETTING

Campsite, late at night. Illumination comes from a campfire, a kerosene lamp and moonlight. There is a tent with the opening facing front, flap hanging down. Camping garb is scattered nearby, sleeping bags as well as sticks and leaves.

Time is the present. Late at night through dawn. A campsite in Upstate New York. During the course of the play the fire and lanterns slowly burn out, the lights slowly rise in the morning.

GHOST STORIES

LIGHTS RISE on ALEX, DODIE and MARGARET sitting around the campfire. They are drinking beer and eating graham crackers, and marshmallows.

DODIE. It started very small, with little knocks and ticks. Getting a chill that you're not alone. Seeing a shadow flash past the corner of your eye but when you turn your head, there's nothing, as if it's already slipped back into the other world.

MARGARET. Get to the good stuff Dodie.

DODIE. One day, she gets home, and finds everything a wreck. Papers everywhere, pictures off the walls, furniture turned over. She doesn't want to stay since whoever did it might be still in there so she runs to get a neighbor.

MARGARET. How can there be neighbors in the middle of nowhere.

DODIE. I didn't say—

MARGARET. Yes, you said—

ALEX. *(interrupts deliberately)* So — she gets some neighbor to come over, right?

DODIE. And he takes one look and says, "Old Buzzie's been at it again."

MARGARET. Buzzie?

DODIE. See, like 50 years ago, Buzzie and his wife had a knock-down-drag-out, tore the place apart and he finally ended up killing her and throwing her body out the window into the sea. Once in a while you hear her screaming as she falls to the bottom of the cliffs.

ALEX. She must have been still alive when he tossed her out the window, and was like — impaled on a rock or something.

MARGARET. Why don't we pick another genre Dodie?

DODIE. I can move the lamp closer—

MARGARET. I'm not scared Do-Do, I just don't think stories about women being thrown out windows is appropriate.

ALEX. She could have bounced down — that would do it.

MARGARET. *(to DODIE)* Don't you agree?

ALEX. What were they fighting about?

DODIE. *(caught between the two)* — um —

ALEX. Wait — no one knows, right? An unsolved mystery. That's why they're ghosts, why they keep coming back. You see — they're trying to show someone, re-enact the truth.

MARGARET. Oh, please Alex.

ALEX. *(to DODIE)* Don't they keep re-enacting the truth?

DODIE. Well, the old man warns her not to stay in the house that night.

MARGARET. But, of course, she ignores his advice, and in the middle of the night, wakes-up and sees, "Oh my God!", a screaming lady being heaved out the window by a ghost named Buzzie.

DODIE. It's true.

MARGARET. It's bull-dinky.

DODIE. I swear it's true.

MARGARET. Your Dad told these stories 15 years ago.

DODIE. That's right, and they're true. *(Meanwhile, ALEX has been making finger puppets in front of her, as if the reflection was out over the audience.)*

MARGARET. What are you doing Alex?

ALEX. *(making puppets)* It's a rooster — see — he's eating inchworms out of the treetops. Give me your hand Dodie. *(She uses DODIE'S hand to make a butterfly.)* Now the rooster's eating a butterfly, see? Close your fingers *(She does, DODIE follows.)* and the butterfly becomes a bat to chase the rooster. Bat—butterfly, butterfly—bat. *(pause)*

MARGARET. Time for another beer. Anybody want another beer?

DODIE. I don't want to have to go to the bathroom out there. I could squat on Poison Ivy.

MARGARET. You're going to have to piss sometime between now and morning.

DODIE. Not if I can help it.

ALEX. I'll take a beer.

MARGARET. *(starts to hand her a beer, stops)* Hey, there isn't any reason you shouldn't drink, medication or something? Mark didn't mention anything.

ALEX. What the hell does Mark know.

MARGARET. I assume he knows whether or not you should drink.

ALEX. Mark doesn't know beans. Mark only knows about Mark. That's his problem.

MARGARET. Well, he must know something since this was his idea.

ALEX. Camping was my idea. He just thought it might be good to get the ol' Musketeers together.

DODIE. And he was right, too, wasn't he? Here we are.

Camping. Are we doing it right?

MARGARET. I haven't the slightest. Everything I'm wearing is borrowed.

ALEX. Don't look at me, I've never done it.

MARGARET. Then, why are we here Alex?

ALEX. I wanted to get back to nature.

MARGARET. And we had to do that in the middle of nowhere New York?

ALEX. *(slightly humoring)* Exactly. Surrounded by green things that grow and breathe in all our bad air, where I can dig down and get dirt and roots under my fingernails and watch . . . ancient mountains of rock and earth stare down at us ants and say, "we were here before you were even a twinkle in a dinosaurs eye!"

DODIE. So ... we're camping. We've all this camping stuff. A fire. Hey, we are — safe, aren't we?

MARGARET. Not from mosquitos. I used that Cutters shit. You'd think smelling like a gas station would be effective. Look — chicken pox. Very attractive.

DODIE. What about — you know — wild animals.

ALEX. It's a campground, wild men's a bit more likely.

MARGARET. Wild men — you'd love that Do-Do.

DODIE. Stop. *(familiar banter)*

ALEX. Speaking of men—

MARGARET. Were we speaking of men?

DODIE. Always.

ALEX. Who's the new guy, Magpie?

DODIE. Yah Magpie, who's the new guy?

MARGARET. Don't call me that. It reminds me of Billy Morse at recess calling me "Mudpie, Magpie".

DODIE. Billy Morse got his though.

ALEX. That's right. You sat on him didn't you. You were a big kid, Do-Do, you almost killed him.

DODIE. Then, you guys made me a musketeer. Squishing Billy Morse was a major turning point in my life.

ALEX. "We're one for all, and all for one" *(She shoves out an imaginary sword, the others follow suit.)* Alex!

MARGARET. Maggie!

DODIE. Sally!

MARGARET. We stopped calling you that fast — on guard I say.

DODIE. I was never very good at this. *(They duel and are interrupted by ALEX singing.)*

ALEX. "Strawberry shortcake cream on top, tell me the name of your sweetheart." *(DODIE has stopped and joined ALEX singing.)*

ALEX/DODIE. "IS IT "A", "B", "C" . . . "D", "E"? . . . "F"?—

ALEX. It's not Xavier is it?

MARGARET. No.

DODIE. Well?

ALEX. *(sings again)* "Maggie and some guy sittin' in a tree. K-I-S-S-I-N-G. First comes love, then comes marriage—

MARGARET. Alright, already. He's not just some guy. He's a professor.

DODIE. Whow, whow. Is he your professor?

MARGARET. He was.

ALEX. Interesting. I can tell you all the things my analyst would say.

MARGARET. This is not what you think. It's very different.

DODIE. What's that — a little father figure stuff?

MARGARET. Hey, you should talk, Do-Do.

DODIE. What do you mean I should talk?

MARGARET. Nothing. Forget it. *(to ALEX)* He's a young, 42, sort of dashing, doctorate in Medieval Studies. Who the hell'd want him as a father. Not when he's that good of a lover.

DODIE. What — I should talk.

MARGARET. By day he stimulates my mind, by night he stimulates my body. I ask you, what more could a girl want?

ALEX. I don't know. I don't know at all. *(DODIE and MARGARET speak at the same time.)*

DODIE. I'm cold, is anybody cold?

MARGARET. Alex, do you want to talk about...

MARGARET. *(finishing)* Do you want to talk?

ALEX. You're cold? Let's throw another stick on. *(She does.)* How come we don't see any other campfires?

MARGARET. All the real campers are asleep by now.

ALEX. What do you say we turn off the lantern. It ruins the effect of the fire.

MARGARET. No way, Jose. I want the street light effect. It helps me forget there's creepy crawlies out there.

DODIE. Not to mention bears.

ALEX. Or wild men.

MARGARET. Anyway — Alex —

ALEX. Tell us about the hometown, Dodie. How's it doing?

DODIE. It's the same pretty much. Jack-n-the-Box became Arby's and Hills Supermarket became Sweezy's department store.

ALEX. I used to go to Hills.

MARGARET. Guess you were the only one.

DODIE. Tuey's closed. So people hang out at Port Jeff or the Park Bench.

ALEX. Is that where you go?

DODIE. I really don't go anywhere.

MARGARET. Why not? You like being there so much. Why don't you socialize with the people?

DODIE. Most of the guys my age are sport junkies who never went to school. What would I say to them?

ALEX. Offer to help them with their taxes.

DODIE. Most of them don't have jobs.

MARGARET. I don't get it, Dodie. You've all the makings of a yuppie. A good education, good career. Why don't you quit that little podunk office, get a job in New York and reap your profits.

DODIE. I can't leave my Dad.

MARGARET. What — is he sick?

DODIE. I don't want to leave him. I'm all he has.

ALEX. God — I almost forgot. *(gets up and runs into tent)*

MARGARET. What do you think?

DODIE. I don't know, what do you think?

MARGARET. We don't get her talking soon it'll be morning.

DODIE. She looks good though huh? I was afraid she'd look weird or — *(ALEX returns. She is holding a pair of Pince-nez glasses that have seen better days.)*

ALEX. Ta-da. I found them in my memory box. Remember? *(There is a pause.)* Come on. Don't you remember?

DODIE. Are we supposed to?

ALEX. Yes, yes! We were in fifth grade.

MARGARET. How about another clue?

ALEX. I can't believe you don't remember. Mom had taken us to Robert Moses. And there was that guy who looked like Popeye with the metal detector.

DODIE. I think I remember — you kept following him around the beach.

ALEX. He had hundreds of metal knick-knacks hanging all over him that he'd found on beaches all over the world.

MARGARET. I must have been off worshipping the sun.

ALEX. We dug these up. I thought they were just broken glasses, but Popeye told me they were pinch noses, worn only by "rich or famous smart people". I thought that was such a great name — pinch noses — Cause that's what they do — pinch your nose. *(pause)* Come on — don't they ring a bell? We thought they were so cool and owned by like Roosevelt or someone — and — and — I brought them home in my sneaker?

DODIE. — yah, of course. *(awkward pause)*

ALEX. Stop looking at me like I've no face.

MARGARET. Sorry. We've just been trying all night not to push you into—

ALEX. *(cuts her off)* Hey, let's hear another ghost story. We used to tell so many, out by the big dirt hole, or my screened-in porch. What was our fascination?

MARGARET. No. No more ghost stories.

ALEX. Yes. Tell us another, Do.

MARGARET. No!

DODIE. I'm still cold. Isn't anybody cold?

MARGARET. Obviously not.

DODIE. Well, I'll just . . . get my sleeping bag. *(She goes into tent.)*

MARGARET. Enough already huh?

ALEX. Enough what?

MARGARET. You said this was your idea, too.

ALEX. That's right. Mine and Mark's.

MARGARET. So then, let's stop playing around and—

ALEX. Did you know that Mark wants me to have a baby?

MARGARET. *(surprised)* Do you?

ALEX. Are you kidding?

MARGARET. It *is* sort of stupid, considering.

ALEX. It's ridiculous, dumb, and so typical. Typical of everything about my life. Completely and horrifiyingly typical. Where do I live? Middletown, New Jersey. Which could just as well be Middletown, Pennsylvania, Illinois, West Virginia, there's one in practically every fucking state with the same fucking houses painted the same putrid colors.

MARGARET. Good — keep going.

ALEX. Oh don't make me puke Mag. You're not my psychiatrist.

MARGARET. I'm just trying to help.

ALEX. Then just be my friend.

MARGARET. O.K. I totally agree. The last thing you need is a baby.

ALEX. I feel like I'm drowning, sucked down the white tornado into my bath tub drain. A tornado I chose to be in. I chose so why do I feel like this?

MARGARET. Do you still love Mark?

ALEX. I don't know. I don't think so.

DODIE. *(coming out of tent with sleeping bag)* I'm sorry, I didn't want to interrupt, but it was so black in there, I'm sorry.

ALEX. Black. Falling into black so fast I'd rather just keep falling than bother making any effort to climb out.

DODIE. I am interrupting. I'll go back in, there's a flashlight somewhere—

MARGARET. *(abruptly harsh)* Stop! and listen with me.

ALEX. *(slight pause)* It's O.K., Do. The moods left me. Have a graham cracker. Let's make smores.

DODIE. Alex — I'm sorry. I've got to ask this. See, I don't understand. You're smart. You're pretty. You've a nice home. A husband who loves you, really loves you. I mean, people would kill to have what you've got.

ALEX. Crazy, huh? What's wrong with this picture? What's rotten in Denmark?

MARGARET. That's not crazy, not everyone wants that.

ALEX. Crazy what I did. Crazy that—

MARGARET. That's why we're here! To help, to listen, whatever you want.

ALEX. Know what I want? To ask you some questions. Is that alright? Please? I've been poked and probed by so many Ph.D's I want to ask my own ... OK? *(DODIE shrugs yes.)*

MARGARET. Just so long as we don't belabor Dodie's days as a porno queen.

DODIE. Oh stop! *(Laughter, tension release.)*

ALEX. What—

MARGARET. Wait. First pass the grahams. *(gets grahams)* O.K. Shoot.

ALEX. What makes you keep going? Everyday?

DODIE. A little Wheaties always does the trick for me. Hey, can't I be funny too?

MARGARET. You're a scream, Do-Do.

ALEX. Well?

MARGARET. Can you elaborate a little?

ALEX. Elaborate — yes, means a bit more explanation.

MARGARET. Come on—

ALEX. O.K. — What after reading your newspaper, history book, fought, spit, cursed at professors, friends, enemies, colleagues, lovers, looked at — the same house, bed, kitchen, garbage on the street, face in the mirror — a thousand disgusted times. What makes you want to get up and be assaulted once again, cause I don't see any reason to bother any more — and maybe I am just sick, but I want to hear from my oldest friends what there is in this life for them. Maybe you'll inspire me.

DODIE. Well.

MARGARET. O.K. then.

DODIE. Let me just think a minute.

ALEX. It's that tough?

MARGARET. No, not at all. It's just hard to come up with your thesis of life off the cuff.

ALEX. I don't want your thesis of life. I want to know what gets you out of bed in the morning.

DODIE. And I really can't get away with food.

ALEX. No bodily functions. Strictly mental.

DODIE. Then — do you want to go, Mag?

MARGARET. I opt to pass.

ALEX. I don't want you thinking about it. I want immediate response.

DODIE. It's O.K. I'll go . . . Alright then. My immediate response was . . . my Dad. Why'd you groan? What's wrong with that? It's true.

MARGARET. Dodie, you and your Dad haven't — forget it. It's too disgusting.

DODIE. What? What?! You . . . you shithead! I can't believe you asked that—

MARGARET. I'm sorry.

DODIE. How could you just say that? Think that? Out loud! Don't you have any feelings any—

MARGARET. Yes I have feelings!

ALEX. Hey, hey, cut it—

DODIE. She asked me if me and—

ALEX. I heard.

MARGARET. I'm really sorry.

ALEX. I think we should just move—

DODIE. No. No, she asked. I'll answer. Has my father ever . . . touched me? No. No one has ever touched me. *(pause)* So, I'll continue with getting out of bed. Dad gets me out of bed, because I know his life would be miserable without me. I have need, I have power. I have a certain type of love. What gets me into the bathroom and brushing my teeth is the potential for the other kind of love. I don't know what it is, really, yet, I can guess, with the help of Dr. Zhivago, Wuthering Heights. It's out there, I've seen it. I've seen it with you and Mark. And one morning I'll have my turn. *(pause)*

MARGARET. Is this we each get three minutes and then there's an informative discussion?

ALEX. When I'm ready to say something, I will. You go.

MARGARET. Well, then. Bringing it all down to one concise sentence. I get up so someday I can say "My fellow Americans, as your President, I feel we should do this..."

DODIE. I get it, you want to be an actress.

MARGARET. I'm very serious. *(beat)*

DODIE. Really? I mean, that's what you really want to be?

MARGARET. When I grow up? This is the first time I've ever told anyone. It's not the kind of thing you bring up in casual conversation.

ALEX. I'm very impressed.

DODIE. Gosh, I don't know anyone — a senator, maybe, but — you can do it, Mags. I know it. Don't you think she can do it?

ALEX. Of course.

DODIE. I'll be able to say — "I knew her when".

ALEX. And that's what keeps you going, huh?

MARGARET. I don't think about—

ALEX. What's your strategy? You've a whole strategy right?

MARGARET. I'm working on degree #2 in Polysci.

ALEX. Is that more important then like — getting a job in the state department?

MARGARET. BA + MA tend to equal respect and proof of brain power. Can't get anywhere without it.

ALEX. Is that why you're dating that professor? Respect and proof of brain power?

MARGARET. Was that an attempt to hit me below the belt?

ALEX. Not at all. I'm just asking if that's why you date your professor.

MARGARET. I told you why I date him. He's interesting, fun and and a good fuck.

ALEX. Haven't I heard that before?

MARGARET. I said this is different.

DODIE. What are you guys talking about?

ALEX. Can I ask you this? How come you never date men your own age?

MARGARET. What makes you think I don't date men my own age?

ALEX. Well, do you?

MARGARET. I've never met anyone I wanted to — older men are —

ALEX. And I bet they don't ask you.

MARGARET. I've been asked—

ALEX. 'Cause they're probably afraid you'll bite their heads off.

DODIE. That's true, you know. You're pretty intimidating.

MARGARET. Shut-up Dodie. *(to ALEX)* What are you trying to say?

ALEX. I don't know. I just want to ask questions. Figure things out. Get this fog out of my eyes! We're out here in the middle of the woods so I can scream and spit. So, let me scream and spit.

MARGARET. Fine. Point yourself in Dodie's direction for awhile.

DODIE. You aren't going to ask me something I don't want to answer are you?

ALEX. No, no. I do have one question though, Do—

DODIE. Let's make smores. Pretend we're girl scouts and—

ALEX. If you're so eager for love, why don't you make any effort to find it?

DODIE. I've got Dad.

ALEX. You're not glued to his knee are you?

DODIE. Of course not.

ALEX. So?

DODIE. I don't have the time.

ALEX. Come on Do.

DODIE. Yes. I commute everyday, it's exhausting.

ALEX. It's only half an hour to Patchogue.

DODIE. Maybe I don't want to.

ALEX. You were dying to date the boys in high school.

DODIE. Maybe I've changed.

MARGARET. Leave her alone.

ALEX. I want her to see—

MARGARET. Let her deal with it, she's obviously not committing—

DODIE. Alright. Want me to say it? I'm scared. I'm scared shitless. Scared I'll break his zipper, fall on my butt. Scared he'll never pick me up, get it up—

(There is a crash off stage. All girls jump.)

DODIE. Now, I'm really scared. *(All listen a moment.)*

MARGARET. Shit! Do you hear anything?

DODIE. It must be a bear. Do we have a manual or something to tell us what to do if it's a bear? *(She starts to rummage through pockets.)*

MARGARET. It's not a bear. Period.

DODIE. *(produces a knife)* Look — I've a jack knife.

MARGARET. What are you going to do, open a bottle?

ALEX. SHHHHH! *(All listen a moment.)*

MARGARET. Why the hell are we here Alex and not at a 4 star hotel in New York City?

ALEX. I wanted to scream and spit.

MARGARET. Go scream and spit at whatever's out there.

ALEX. It was probably just a tree.

MARGARET. Who chopped it down? The jolly green giant?

ALEX. Trees can fall by themselves. *(She walks to the edge of the lights.)* Anyone out there? Hello? Anybody there? *(pause)* I'm sure it was just a tree. *(turns and looks at others)* You guys look like you just saw Buzzie throw his wife out the window.

DODIE. I wish we had, then we'd know what it was.

ALEX. I can go out and find it.

MARGARET. What makes you so brave, Miss Suburban American Princess? You don't know anything about the woods. I know you don't. Who knows what could be out there.

DODIE. *(fast)* Snakes, rats, wolves, bigfoot—

ALEX. You think this is scary? This is nothing. A little tingling in my toes. Adrenaline to remind me for some reason my heart's still beating. Want to know scary?

MARGARET. Alex—

ALEX. Once upon a time there was a girl who was sure she lived in a haunted house because everytime she walked into a room, she'd see a completely different place that had totally different furniture — a den looking like a dorm room, a kitchen like an office, til she was terrified to walk into a room for fear she would be lost, or in some other plane where rooms had minds of their own.

MARGARET. Please Alex, sit down and—

ALEX. Sit down hell. It didn't take the girl long to figure out it was she who was haunted by the ghost of what could have been, who taunted her with flashes of whole other lives, lives that never would happen because, you see, she chose who she was. What if you never went to that football game, took that class, said yes to that —man, maybe there would have been more choices, and other lives lost. And when all those images started pounding on her brain, the ghost of the wrong choice took over, every moment reminding her that this was what you wanted, and if he isn't what you thought love meant, it's not all this wonderful world you dreamed about then tough shit you made the choice. *(MARGARET attempts to stand, ALEX stops her.)* NO, you just sit there and listen. That's when she realized she was the ghost — yes, I was nothing but a ghost walking through the day climbing into my grave at night only to walk the earth in the morning. Everyday only existed to get me through to the next, and the next and the next. I'd grab chunks of my skin, only there were no nerves. I was just a shell, but inside my mind was screaming! I had to save myself, prove I wasn't a ghost. I was *real.* So, after Mark hussled away with his morning bran flakes and brown lunch bag, I went upstairs, and instead of putting his razor away, I took it apart. Funny, it had one of those double edged blades, and I actually wrapped the one edge with tissue paper so I wouldn't cut my fingers while I was attempting to slice my wrist.

DODIE. I can't listen to this.

ALEX. It's not easy you know, one quick little flick doesn't do it. It's slippy and messy, but I kept going cause once I saw red — felt the red, I knew I wasn't a ghost. See, I'm alive. I can prove it. Look! I'm real!!

MARGARET. O.K., let's all just—

ALEX. See, it wasn't until I woke up and found nothing had changed that I really panicked. Here I was sure I had exorcised all those demons from my head — washed them away with all that red. But they were all still there. The school I never finished, my silly part-time job, the love I thought would shower me for a lifetime. It's not his fault! He's just not enough for me — me who is *nothing.* One of many nondescript, horribly average ordinary humans who have no reason for being except maybe consumption and reproduction — Lemmings who could go run off a cliff and the world wouldn't be any worse by it. Do you see? What's the use? What's the fucking use of it all!? *(bolts off into the woods)*

MARGARET. *(jumps up)* Alex stop! Shit! SHIT! *(starts to go after her, quickly addresses DODIE)* You stay, if she doubles back, keep her here.

DODIE. What if I can't?

MARGARET. Sit on her. *(turns, runs off)*

DODIE. *(alone)* I'm so scared. I wish I was home in my

bed . . . with the lights on. *(looks out)* Everything's fine, everything's fine . . . now I lay me down to sleep, I pray the Lord my soul to keep, If I die before I wake—

(ALEX comes running in.)

ALEX. *(laughing)* You should see Mags.

DODIE. Where is she?

ALEX. I left her in the dust. Then she tripped over a tent.

DODIE. Why'd you run off like that?

ALEX. I wanted to.

(MARGARET enters very spooked.)

MARGARET. Don't you ever do that to me again — as long as you live — *never.* I couldn't see a damn thing. Just all those trees coming out of fucking nowhere, branches smashing into my face — didn't know where I was, where you'd gone. What if there was a cliff? What if that tent was full of — what were you trying to prove!

ALEX. I can still run faster than you?

MARGARET. I come all the way up here to help you. It's not like I had nothing better to do.

ALEX. Why don't you go then, no one's keeping you. You've got things to do, the State Department's waiting.

MARGARET. I feel like saying I told you so! You go on about the wrong choices — I'm the one who said—

ALEX. I know what you said. You wore it on a sandwich board at the wedding.

MARGARET. And I was right!

DODIE. No, you're not. She and Mark were in love. That's all that matters.

MARGARET. God, I'm so sick of the word love being treated like some precious jewel, a glass bubble that makes everything utopia. I hate it.

ALEX. You would.

MARGARET. Love is a bunch of gauze.

ALEX. You whose major love affairs have been with some Harvard professor and Mr. Griffiths.

DODIE. You had an affair with Mr. Griffiths!?

MARGARET. Oh, beautiful.

DODIE. God, isn't he kinda old — cute, but, we were in high school.

MARGARET. Christ, Alex, why'd you—

ALEX. Did that have anything to do with love?

MARGARET. What if I'm not looking for love? What if I'm looking for lust? Maybe I don't need it. It would just get in my way.

ALEX. That's right. My pal the iceberg.

MARGARET. *Don't* start—

DODIE. I know you want love, everyone does. It's something chemical that your body can't function normally without — that's why if you don't have it you think about it practically every moment and stare at every man who passes you on the street to see if he's the one — if some instant electrical response joins our eyes and our hands. Cause then, when you have love, you can do anything! Climb the Empire State Building with one hand. What you have to do Mags is let that right guy into your life. Let that electrical response happen.

MARGARET. What in god's name do you know about

love? You're just fantasizing what it's like to have a lover — a husband. Maybe it's not all fireworks. Maybe it sucks, maybe it's not enough.

DODIE. I do know what it's like.

ALEX. Didn't you say you've never been touched?

DODIE. I lied.

MARGARET. What do you mean you lied?

DODIE. I lied. Someone has touched me. All over.

ALEX. This isn't anything bad — you weren't—

DODIE. He was an engine major, my lab partner. And a face — god, my whole body shook when he looked at me. Nothing — none of my crushes in high school made me feel like this. I had to do something to make him look at me as more than just his lab partner. Don't get me wrong, he didn't think I was a boring braino, we'd have coffee after class, laugh — all that. But I was still Dodie from class. One evening, we were supposed to meet at his apartment to exchange notes. I went to him in an imitation fur coat — and a diaphragm. That's it.

MARGARET. There's no way this is true.

DODIE. I knocked, walked in...

MARGARET. You wouldn't do this, I wouldn't do this.

DODIE. ...asked if anyone was here or if he was expecting anyone. And when he said no, I dropped the coat.

ALEX. My god, you really did do this.

DODIE. He was a bit surprised having expected me to hand him a lab book. It was my one seductive act.

MARGARET. Never in a million years...

ALEX. Don't just stop. What happened!!

Margaret. He didn't want to do it.

Alex. *(guessing)* He had a girlfriend, he was gay?

Dodie. No, we did it.

Margaret. You did it!

Alex. And he has horrible, clumsy, bang, bang rollover.

Dodie. No. It was really good.

Alex. So, then, I don't get it.

Dodie. Well . . . he never called me.

Margaret. But, he was your partner, you cornered him in cl—

Dodie. He dropped the class.

Margaret. Oh, schmuck, schmuck, dirt bag...

Dodie. So, I guess it wasn't as good as I thought. I sort of lost confidence . . . never done it again.

Margaret. ...rotten, slimey, scummy...

Alex. Oh, D, you never should have kept that in.

Margaret. ...putrid piece of turd.

Alex. You should have told us.

Dodie. I couldn't, it sounds so slutty — the fur coat.

Alex. It's not at all, it's wonderfully sexy, erotic — daring.

Dodie. Then why didn't he call?

Alex. Because obviously he's an asshole and he made you run back to Stonybrook and bury your head in the sand.

Margaret. Not to mention your—

Dodie. Just stop! I told you the story, now just leave me alone.

Alex. But Do, sweetie, we just want you to see why

you're scared, why you're holding on to your dad with both hands.

DODIE. Shut-up about him.

ALEX. So you can get out.

DODIE. Shut-up.

ALEX. I know it's painful.

DODIE. Shut-up, shut up, what's wrong with being close to my father? You're all just jealous, jealous cause I've got it so good.

ALEX. You don't really believe that — I know you too well. You haven't always been Daddy's Dodie.

DODIE. What am I supposed to do? Huh? I'm not like you. I'm not pretty. Not funny. I didn't have the pick of every boy in the entire high school. And I don't have this blinding ambition that turns on older men, I mean, could you see me dating Mr. Griffiths? I know what you're trying to tell me. I'm not *blind.* Just tell me what I'm supposed to do. I can't take that rejection again. I'd rather just be at home cause I know at least—

ALEX. You've just got to be brave again. That's all. You've done it before right? And if someone isn't interested — ha — too bad — it's their loss. Because you're spectacular. We wouldn't have let you be a musketeer if you weren't. Just start small. Pretend you're that girl who stayed and saw Buzzie and his wife. She was warned, but it's her house, so what those ghosts can't let go of it. They're dead — gone. She's the one that's alive. That's right, she's alive . . . and they're just ghosts.

MARGARET. I've had enough of this ghost stuff. It's just a little too freaky with the woods, why we're here. We should just get down to business. Don't you think,

Dodie? Just figure out what Alex should do from here. I've been thinking about it — I've a few ideas. I'm sure you do.

ALEX. They can't let go of it, even if they wanted to. They have to keep re-enacting the truth. They're stuck, held.

DODIE. Who's stuck?

ALEX. Buzzie and his wife.

MARGARET. Cut the ghost crap, please Alex.

ALEX. Sorry — what?

MARGARET. We were figuring out what you should do. Therapy's not helping anymore, it seems.

ALEX. ...not really, no.

MARGARET. Your doctors weren't a bunch of quacks, I presume.

ALEX. No...

MARGARET. So, what do you think, Do?

DODIE. I don't know — are you alright, Alex?

ALEX. Sure . . . yeh.

MARGARET. O.K. I've a couple of ideas. First, is to really find your personal goal. What you want to accomplish in the next 50 odd years.

ALEX. Goals? What goals? I want to *understand.* Why. Why I keep coming back, can't leave it alone. Why I kept calling myself a ghost, why we spent a 100 hours on my porch scaring ourselves to death about souls that couldn't let go of the earth. There's a key. There has to be.

MARGARET. You've got to have a goal or you'll never get—

ALEX. No — it's more, Mags. Something so much

more . . . so vital, so incredibly wonderful about *life* that we have ghosts at *all.* That makes them stay and haunt, hold on to whatever shred of life they can still possibly grab. There's some reason...

DODIE. What is that reason? *(pause)*

ALEX. I don't know. I haven't the slightest. But do you see, I want to know. I want to find it. It exists somewhere on this planet. I just found the first piece to the puzzle. There's probably 200 more but I've started. God! It's suddenly so clear! There must be something about the world, no matter how crappy it is, how miserable, that makes them cling with only their spirits. It has to be so glorious. So worth having life.

DODIE. You really believe that? You're really—

ALEX. Yes, yes. I've this one piece in my hand, and it'll lead me to the next and the next until finally the puzzle's complete. I just need to figure out where to begin.

MARGARET. I know.

DODIE. You do?

MARGARET. Of course. For starters, you have to get the hell out of New Jersey and away from Mark. You don't love him.

DODIE. Now wait, that's not true—

MARGARET. You don't love him and the place almost put you out of your misery. Where you can start again . . . is with me. I want you to come back to school with me. It's so, absolutely perfect. Where else but a university with intellectual people discussing, arguing exactly what made you crazy. You could live with me. Get a job in town, start with one or two classes, then take a full load in the fall.

ALEX. What makes you think I'll get in?

MARGARET. I date a professor, remember? Alex, it would be a whole new road. One of those lives you thought you'd never have but you will. I'll take care of you, I want to.

DODIE. How do you know she doesn't want to work things out with Mark?

MARGARET. I don't get you — we just found out the love of your life was a schmuck, you'd think you'd be pushing her out of Middletown with both feet.

DODIE. I can still recognize a good thing even if I don't have it.

MARGARET. You call her life good? *(ALEX has meanwhile crossed away. She looks at woods, listening intently away from the conversation.)*

DODIE. She should at least give it a chance—

MARGARET. No, now's the time. A clean break. Get the bus from Albany straight to Boston. There's one at 7. We should just get out of the woods and back to the world. That's where we belong. Out there with people who can make a difference, fix this fucked-up world.

DODIE. And who's going to meet Mark at Port Authority?

MARGARET. You.

DODIE. No way, I can't, who do you think I—

MARGARET. A gutsy lady who can seduce a man with her birthday suit and a fur. You want to be brave, here's your start.

ALEX. SHHHH!

(All quiet. The lights at this point should just be breaking dawn.

The fire is out, the lantern burned down.)

ALEX. Listen, hear it?

MARGARET. Hear what?

ALEX. Dawn.

MARGARET. You can't—

ALEX. Yes! You could be blind but you'd still know. A new day. *(after a moment)* I'm not going with you, Margaret.

MARGARET. Why not?

ALEX. I don't want to.

MARGARET. What — well, what the hell else are you going to do?

ALEX. Stay here.

MARGARET. Here? In the woods?

ALEX. For a while anyway.

MARGARET. It's ridiculous. You're crazy.

ALEX. I'm very sane. I've got a tent. Warm clothes, enough cash to survive. I'll work my way around, talk to people, different people. The type you don't meet in Long Island or New Jersey.

MARGARET. You want to travel, fine. We'll do it in the summer. It'll be fun.

ALEX. Don't you get it! All my life I have been perfectly safe. Always had a nice house to come home to with a nicely stocked frig or at least a Pizza Hut around the corner and two cars to get me there. I was a ghost! But now I've got my hands on the key. I know who I am right *now*. I've got to find what this key opens. I've been to school, it's not the answer.

MARGARET. You're totally wrong. You were walking

around in a daze because your brain had become play dough. And it's going to stay that way unless you give it some stimulation.

ALEX. But, that's what I'm doing. If anything, you should come with me.

MARGARET. What do you mean?

ALEX. In fact, that's a good idea. You should come with me.

MARGARET. And stay here in the woods?

ALEX. Not just here — the smokey mountains, the salt flats, the desert.

MARGARET. We can travel in the summer!

ALEX. Not as tourists, as people meeting different people — looking for the pieces to the puzzle.

MARGARET. This is crazy, dumb. You think I should leave school to go wander around America.

ALEX. Yes.

MARGARET. Why?

ALEX. I don't want you to miss out.

MARGARET. Miss out what? — you're the one that's missing out. I'm offering you a chance to be a part of an incredible community of—

ALEX. And I'm offering you a chance to really learn, to see—

MARGARET. You're telling me I don't—

ALEX. Stopping, and looking at life rather than plowing through it.

MARGARET. Now, wait a minute.

ALEX. I don't know what we'll find. But there's some reason for it all.

MARGARET. Just what are you saying?

ALEX. This is how you can melt the iceberg.

MARGARET. I said don't start.

ALEX. I'm just trying to help.

MARGARET. I'm not the one with the problem! The idea is you come with me to help your problem.

ALEX. And I say we do it the other way around.

MARGARET. We don't need to do it the other way around! Let's get this straight here on who needs assistance. We were both taught from age two there's nothing wrong with knowing who you are what you want and trying to get it. It's ranked right up there with apple pie.

ALEX. And you really know all that?

MARGARET. Yes, god dammit. And what the hell do you think you're going to find? Bopping around truck-stops with nothing to show for it but a bunch of greyhound tickets!

ALEX. I don't know. God? An answer?

MARGARET. I'm the one who's going to accomplish something, move legislation. Push us forward.

DODIE. What's this iceberg stuff?

MARGARET. We've got to be strong. All of us. Intellectually, economically. That's the answer. There's no other way.

ALEX. *(to DODIE)* Iceberg is just a name.

MARGARET. That's right. A little name Alex coined for me.

ALEX. From an accident, that's all.

MARGARET. Go ahead tell it.

ALEX. I don't want to.

MARGARET. Well. Fine. Then I will. 11th grade. We're walking down my driveway and I feel this . . . squish under my shoe . . . and I just thought damn, dog do. So I stop, look down — and see this - - - baby bird . . . just . . . all over my shoe. All I want to do is get it off, get it off! I grab a stick to scrape it off. Fling it away, far away. But Alex saw, called me an iceberg . . . and made me stand there and watch as she gave it a little fucking funeral! GOD! I just wanted to scream!

ALEX. Come on! Get on a bus with me and meet real people who aren't brilliant or published.

MARGARET. I can't stop.

ALEX. Why not?

MARGARET. I can't. It's the only thing I have. My protection so I don't end up bleeding all over the bathroom floor like you. Is that what you want to see? Another bleeding mess? That's not going to happen to me. I'm strong. I have a brain and I'm going to use it! No one's getting inside and destroying my hopes — tell me they can't be. I've seen it happen. To my mother, to her mother. All around me. To you, my best friend. That's why I'm never going to stop. I'm going to get somewhere. And if that means fucking a 42 year old child who calls himself a professor, I will. I'll use his position, burn off a little excess tension, and when I'm through, climb right over him. And I won't care, I'll be strong.

ALEX. And when you get to that last rung, you're going to look around and say, so fucking what!

MARGARET. No!

ALEX. Nothing but clouds.

MARGARET. No. It'll be wonderful. I'll be way up there, way above the world where I can look down and say —

look what I've done, everyone. Aren't you proud of me? *(MARGARET is silent. Then quickly gathers her pack.)*

DODIE. Where are you going?

MARGARET. I'm getting that 7 o'clock bus. This is your last chance. Are you coming with me?

ALEX. ...no.

MARGARET. *(pause)* Fine, then. It's your fucking life. *(to DODIE)* Maybe I'll see you, Do. *(She exits.)*

DODIE. Boy, she's right, you know?

ALEX. What, Dodie?

DODIE. Sally. My name is Sally, remember?

ALEX. I remember.

DODIE. God. God! You know what? I'm hot shit. I am. I must be if I could do that, right? Talk about guts. I seduced the man of my dreams. Who the hell can say they did that?

ALEX. Not many.

DODIE. When I get home, I'm going to give my dad a big hug, then I'm going out the door, no matter what he says, and go straight to the Park Bench and give the first cute guy I see a smack on the lips that'll knock his socks off. *(She starts to gather her stuff.)*

ALEX. You're getting that bus?

DODIE. I've got to catch Mark off guard. Keep him from sending a posse after you. I don't know what I'll say yet. But I'll think of something. And you know what? I will too!

ALEX. So, I shouldn't go back to the comforts of love in New Jersey?

DODIE. Hey, it's your fucking life.

ALEX. Bye, Sally.

DODIE. Right. Sally. I've got to get everyone to start calling me Sally. *(She waves goodbye. DODIE exits. ALEX is left alone. She is quiet a moment. Then, slowly smiles. Starts to rebuild the fire.)*

End of play.

PROPERTY/SET PIECE LIST

ONSTAGE:

Tent
Campfire
Rock (large enough to be sat on)
Three sleeping bags (one in tent)
One blanket
Three backpacks:
- In Dodie's:
  - Earmuffs
  - Mittens
  - Swiss Army Knife
  - Teddybear
  - Misc. camping clothes
- In Margaret's:
  - Clutch purse
  - Cigarette/lighter
  - Cutters Insect Repellent
  - Misc. camping clothes
- In Alex's: (in tent)
  - Pince-nez
  - Misc. camping clothes

Bag of marshmallows
Box of Graham Crackers
Box of chocolate
Six-pack of beer
Lantern
Empty bucket of Kentucky Fried Chicken
Scattered leaves and sticks

SOUND

Crickets and woods sounds (opening)
Offstage tree crash

FLOOR PLAN

Campfire, C.S. Two sleeping bags and rock surrounding campfire. Lantern on top of over-turned Kentucky Fried Chicken Bucket, U.L. Tent, U.R. Dodie's bag, D.L. Margaret's bag, six-pack of beer, D.R. Scattered leaves and sticks.

COSTUME PLOT

MARGARET

Borrowed safari outfit (jacket, pants, boots)
Scarf
Beret

DODIE

Pink sweatpants
Mickey Mouse sweatshirt
Sneakers
(Earmuffs and mittens)

ALEX

Nice jeans
Down vest
Turtleneck
LL Bean duck shoes
Pearls

Other Publications for Your Interest

THE SQUARE ROOT OF LOVE

(ALL GROUPS—FOUR COMEDIES)

By DANIEL MELTZER

1 man, 1 woman—4 Simple Interiors

This full-length evening portrays four preludes to love—from youth to old age, from innocence to maturity. Best when played by a single actor and actress. **The Square Root of Love.** Two genius-level college students discover that Man (or Woman) does not live by intellectual pursuits alone . . . **A Good Time for a Change.** Our couple are now a successful executive and her handsome young male secretary. He has decided it's time for a change, and so has she . . . **The Battling Brinkmires.** George and Marsha Brinkmire, a middle-aged couple, have come to Haiti to get a "quickie" divorce. This one has a surprise ending . . . **Waiting For To Go.** We are on a jet waiting to take off for Florida. He's a retired plumbing contractor who thinks his life is over—she's a recent widow returning to her home in Hallandale. The play, and the evening, ends with a beginning . . . A success at off-off Broadway's Hunter Playwrights. Requires only minimal settings. (#21314)

SNOW LEOPARDS

(LITTLE THEATRE—COMIC DRAMA)

By MARTIN JONES

2 women—Exterior

This haunting little gem of a play was a recent crowd-pleaser Off Off Broadway in New York City, produced by the fine StageArts Theatre Co. Set in Lincoln Park Zoo in Chicago in front of the snow leopards' pen, the play tells the story of two sisters from rural West Virginia. When we first meet Sally, she has run away from home to find her big sister Claire June, whose life Up North she has imagined to be filled with all the promise and hopes so lacking Down Home. Turns out, life in the Big City ain't all Sally and C.J. thought it would be: but Sally is going to stay anyway, and try to make her way. "Affecting and carefully crafted . . . a moving piece of work."—New York City Tribune. *Actresses take note*: this play is a treasure trove of scene and monologue material. *Producers take note*: the play may be staged simply and inexpensively. (#21245)